Praise for *Can Ireland Be One?*

'This book will quickly become essential ~~~~~~ for anyone who speaks about Ireland ~ ~ ~, London, Brussels or Washingto~ ~ ~ will either be constantly nodding ~ ~ a greater complexity than you im~ ~~~ng Ireland is a fascinating place.'

John, Lord Alderdice, FRCPsych, Senior Research Fellow,
Harris Manchester College, University of Oxford

'Engaging, illuminating and never afraid to challenge shibboleths on all sides, *Can Ireland Be One?* unpicks the complexities of the issues set to dominate any border poll in Northern Ireland. Malachi O'Doherty expertly weaves together reportage, political and cultural history and his own family roots in this lucid assessment of what's at stake for people on both sides of the Irish border.'

Mark Devenport, Broadcaster, Commentator,
former BBC NI Political Editor

'A riveting read! By skillfully de-mythologising the narratives upon which our conflict has thrived, Malachi challenges us, whatever our intuitive or inherited position on Irish unity, to objectively consider the realties central to this debate. How can we accommodate the legitimate aspiration of some and avoid the redistribution of resentment of others? A dispassionate contribution to a conversation which will increasingly demand our attention. A conversation which must be about our future rather than our past.'

Harold Good, former President of the Methodist Church

'As a border poll on Irish unity has progressed from possible, to likely, to certain, Malachi O'Doherty's book represents an important and timely contribution to a debate which will probably dominate Irish politics for the next few years. As he notes, the key issues (particularly that of an Irish identity) need addressed and resolved long in advance of any constitutional reboot.'

Alex Kane, newspaper columnist and political commentator

'A well-considered, deeply personal and thought-provoking exploration on that timely question: *Can Ireland be One?* O'Doherty seamlessly moves between Northern Ireland's complicated past and its potential futures from many perspectives, including the often-overlooked new migrants and historically marginalised people. This lively and engaging text cuts through the propaganda to demonstrate why it's complicated.'

Laura McAtackney, Associate Professor in the Department of Archaeology and Heritage Studies, Aarhus University

'A captivating examination of what it means to be Irish, or to feel Irish. Infused with his own personal journey throughout, O'Doherty's timely work assesses the prospects for Irish unity, amidst increasing momentum for a border poll, courtesy of Brexit. In this thought-provoking work, O'Doherty delves into his own 'undecideness' and leaves the reader pondering the deciding factors that will be foremost in voters' minds as they eventually make their historic mark for or against Irish unity.'

Dr Marisa McGlinchey, Assistant Professor of Political Science, Coventry University

'A salutary puncture wound to the easy myth that a United Ireland benignly lies just around the corner and that the complexities of British–Irish identities can wished away.'

Kevin Toolis, journalist and filmmaker

CAN IRELAND BE ONE?

Malachi O'Doherty is a writer and broadcaster based in Belfast, a columnist for the *Belfast Telegraph* and a frequent contributor to several radio programmes as a respected commentator on Northern Ireland. His last book for Merrion was a novel, *Terry Brankin Has a Gun*. It was hailed by critics as 'a superb thriller'. Malachi was awarded a PhD in Creative Writing by Queen's University Belfast and has received a Major Artist Award from the Arts Council of Northern Ireland.

Also by Malachi O'Doherty

The Trouble With Guns (The Blackstaff Press, 1998)

I Was A Teenage Catholic (Marino, 2003)

The Telling Year: Belfast 1972 (Gill & Macmillan, 2007)

Empty Pulpits (Gill & Macmillan, 2008)

Under His Roof (Summer Palace Press, 2009)

On My Own Two Wheels (The Blackstaff Press, 2012)

Gerry Adams: An Unauthorised Life (Faber, 2017)

Fifty Years On: The Troubles and the Struggle for Change in Northern Ireland (Atlantic Books, 2019)

Terry Brankin Has A Gun (Merrion Press, 2020)

The Year of Chaos: Northern Ireland on the Brink of Civil War, 1971/72 (Atlantic Books, 2021)

CAN IRELAND BE ONE?

MALACHI O'DOHERTY

MERRION
PRESS

First published in 2022 by
Merrion Press
10 George's Street
Newbridge
Co. Kildare
Ireland
www.merrionpress.ie

978 1 78537 303 9 (Paper)
978 1 78537 352 7 (Ebook)

A CIP catalogue record for this book is
available from the British Library.

Typeset in Minion Pro 11.5/16.5 pt

Cover image: Detail from Ptolemy's Prima Europe tabula, courtesy of
Llyfrgell Genedlaethol Cymru – The National Library of Wales
Cover design by kvaughan.com

Merrion Press is a member of Publishing Ireland.

For Maureen

CONTENTS

PROLOGUE

IT WAS EASTER Sunday, 10 April 1966. I was in Casement Park GAA ground in Belfast, not to see a match but waiting in the stand among a few hundred others for a parade coming up the Falls Road to mark the half centenary of the Easter Rising. It was a bright, sunny afternoon.

We were all there to remember the day in 1916 when revolutionaries declared Ireland a free and independent republic. They proclaimed themselves to be the legitimate government of the whole island and presumed to act on behalf of all the people; a people they imagined to be of one mind in their determination to shake off government by Britain, a people whose allegiance they believed themselves entitled to claim. Yet what those revolutionaries had dreamed of had not come into being. One part of Ireland had declared itself a republic, in keeping to some extent with that vision, but six counties in the north were sectioned off and governed by unionists as part of Britain still. That's where we were.

We were on Gaelic ground within the British North, a space where the Irish tricolour could fly without interference though the law forbade its display in public. We in the stand were largely motivated by a concern not just to honour our martyrs, but to urge that their work be completed so that the whole of our divided island might be united into a single free nation under this one flag.

At least, that's what I thought we were there for.

My friend John was on the pitch with a large tricolour, enjoying the mischief and daring of waving it in front of an audience of men and women who were merely waiting, their attention easily caught. John held the pole in both hands and swung the flag in front of him so that it caught the breeze and spread and shimmered as he spun, and he chanted his defiance of injustice and oppression, himself now, in his own head anyway, a warrior for Ireland. His exultation and patriotism were contained in the one word that he roared out over and over again. That word was: Celtic! Celtic! Celtic!

And this confused me.

I was fifteen. I didn't care much for football, but I saw the anomaly in celebrating a soccer team on a GAA pitch. GAA members were banned from playing soccer. So many rules!

My patriotism was bound up with my reverence for that flag and my love of the poetry of Patrick Pearse. I could recite much of it by heart. The words Pearse had attributed to his mother the night before he and his brother Willie were executed by firing squad were vindicated as prophecy this very day:

> They shall be spoken of among their people,
> The generations shall remember them …

John's patriotism expressed itself in support for a Scottish football team.

And the patriotism of the men and women in the stands around me? Farmers, business-folk, teachers, solicitors, priests, publicans and council workers. What brought the passion for a united Ireland into sharp focus for them? The preservation of the faith? The Gaelic language? The price of land or cattle? The finishing of unfinished business?

I couldn't say.

But for the first time I wondered if it might be something different for everybody, if we were united at all by anything other than a determination to have a united Ireland. And what would unite us afterwards if we got that? I'm still asking that question.

1

IN THE BEGINNING

I WAS BORN by the border. That was when that border was only thirty years old, in 1951. My father's mother was a native Irish speaker from north Donegal. I know very little about my father's father, other than that the census does not describe him as an Irish speaker and I never in my life heard my own father, his son, speak a word of it. They were from the part of Ireland closest to the Arctic Circle. It suffers bleak and hazardous Atlantic winters, where the trees grow bent against the bitter wind, yet I have had glorious summer holidays there, when the stronger climatic influences were from the south.

Ireland sits between climate zones and seems positioned by geography to be a point of division, a boundary or perhaps a connection. We huddle against storms that would daunt the Inuit and bask in occasional Mediterranean summers. We have palm trees on the western coast. Schools close for snow and occasionally the tarmac melts in the summer, so reconciling ourselves to extremes should be in our nature. It isn't.

We call this climate temperate or moderate. It is, in fact, bi-polar. But we are so little adjusted to that reality that season swings actually surprise us. A coming storm will make headline news and we will be little prepared for it, as if we have never seen the likes of it before. We don't learn.

We are different from the Swiss or the Austrians. They know what weather to expect. They know what clothes to wear for the cold: fully zippered puff jackets. We don't. We still put our faith in wool. Sure it's good enough for the sheep that shiver on the hills and that deliriously wander the country roads. But wool holds the rain. I walked to school as a child in short trousers with the soaked hem of my woollen duffel coat rubbing the backs of my knees and giving me a rash.

My mother's father was an O'Halloran from County Cork, the most southerly part of Ireland, where the climate is more clement. William O'Halloran was a seaman, at first on sailing ships. A chief petty officer in the Royal Navy, like tens of thousands of other Irish men, he was serving Britain even before the great clash of empires of the First World War. This was before Patrick Pearse and Éamon de Valera had redefined Ireland as Gaelic and Catholic, before the narrative had fully taken hold that Ireland was a rebel colony that had long been stripped of its freedom and had to fight its way back to being a nation once again.

Granda was of a type with Sebastian Barry's Steward of Christendom, the British official before independence who was content to serve the Union, but there were rebels in his line too. One was deported to Van Diemen's Land in the 1850s. If I google the O'Hallorans of Tasmania today, I find a road named after his people, and a contemporary of my grandfather with the same name listed among the Great War veterans. That William O'Halloran is recorded as having missed out on the Battle of the Somme because of a spinal injury caused by sleeping awkwardly on his arm. 'I've heard some excuses' is what my old form master Brother Walshe, also a Cork man, would have said to that. The Australian William O'Halloran was returned to the Front in time to be killed at Le Sars.

My mother's mother was a Lane and a devout Irish Catholic. She, too, was from a naval family and Granda met her in Plymouth, where my mother was later born. During the War of Independence, they moved to Ireland. It was just after the end of the Great War and millions of people were seeking to repair disrupted lives. He was thirty-eight years old and had a wife and child, so he would not be going to sea again. He joined the coastguard in Annalong, County Down, at the foot of the Mournes, one of the quietest spots in Ireland in those troubled times. He showed no apparent desire to be part of the new Irish state and settled on the British side of the border by choice. Granda had a later posting to the coastguard in Ballycastle and retired there.

My grannie was made a secretary of the British Legion in Ballycastle. She is remembered as having been conservative and religious. When giving out charity, she would prefer to give food, such as a bag of sugar, rather than cash that could be squandered on cigarettes or drink. She's not to be blamed for not knowing that sugar is bad for you. Other people didn't know that at the time either.

Granda had his British pension and a cottage on the Coleraine road, with the long acre at the back where he could grow his own vegetables. I played in his garden as a child, but he warned me not to sniff the poppies or they would give me a headache. Only now do I think to wonder if those flowers had symbolic value for him as one who had come through war.

My aunt Peg, their second daughter, left an account of her life growing up in Ballycastle and she says that though her mother, my grannie O'Halloran, grew up in Devonshire, England, her parents 'were both completely Irish in background'. And that phrase intrigues me – 'completely Irish'. My grandparents' Irishness did not exclude them from also being British, at least British enough to fight Britain's wars and raise charitable funds for British veterans.

So what is it to be 'completely Irish'? I know what it is like to be regarded as incompletely Irish, because we northerners fear that that is how we are seen by people in the South. And the northern Catholic culture in which I grew up has many terms for the one who is regarded as having a diluted commitment to Irish identity: the Castle Catholic, the souper, the West Brit. The presumption behind such jibes is that there is a right way and a wrong way to be Irish, that obligations come with the fact of having been born on the island or of Irish stock abroad. I've had those jibes thrown at me for expressing views not consistent with the nationalist programme, the inherited story. But this narrow conception of Irishness ignores real-life complexities and it is those complexities which most intrigue me.

*

I was born in Donegal, not a mile from the house my father and his siblings grew up in, though in another country. My father was a little boy of seven when customs posts and checkpoints were erected just yards from his family home. He must have taken it as a personal violation, a new limit to how far he could ride on his trike along a country coastal road. That meandering line, first drawn in Elizabethan times as a county boundary, now cut Ireland in two, leaving his family on the British side, complicating their relationship with the territory they were most familiar with: Donegal to the north and west.

My parents lived, when I was born, in a little village called Muff, the name anglicised from Magh. There is a harp on my birth certificate, but when I was less than two years old my family moved to Ballycastle, to a new house on a small estate round the corner from my O'Halloran grandparents. So I grew up in Northern Ireland, or the North as many say, denying the region the right to a distinctive name.

The move to Ballycastle enabled us to get a nice house and to benefit from a more generous welfare system. My mother had her fifth child in Ballycastle and needed that support, as well as the proximity to her own parents. Later, civil rights agitation would erupt over discrimination in housing allocation, but we were not discriminated against.

My grandparents in the O'Doherty and O'Halloran strands of the family had both crossed borders. In the present generation of my extended family there are cousins in the Republic, in Scotland, in Canada and the United States. My nephews and nieces are in the north of England and, on my wife's side, in the home counties and spreading out from there. If we were a flower, you would say that we thrive in many soil types.

Although my father never once in his life left the island of Ireland, his sister Ena married in Scotland and I have cousins there who have Scottish accents and British passports but still regard themselves as Irish and come 'home' for funerals. Cousin Hugh, who's about my own age, is a member of the Rotary Club and has toasted the Queen at a dinner on a Trident submarine. 'It goes over my head; it doesn't bother me,' he says. He is both Irish and British without difficulty. Hugh would not vote for Scottish independence, yet he would love to see a united Ireland. I suppose the consistency in that is an aversion to borders dividing island landmasses.

His children feel barely Irish at all. He thinks the Irish in Scotland are at home there, but in a way, they could not be at home in the southeast of England. There are varieties of Britishness as there are varieties of Irishness and there is no precise dividing line between them, though some types of each are poles apart.

The organic links between Scotland and Donegal are strong, through a long history of marriages made in Glasgow and Edinburgh by young nurses and teachers who left small farms and villages for work there, or from navvies who built the roads and railways and brought wives home with them. The SDLP leader, John Hume, had the insight that the real border in Ireland is a division of people rather than territory. I think he might have extended that insight to describe the connections and divisions between the Irish in Donegal and in Scotland, between the Irish whose forebears fought for the Empire and whose own siblings fought for the Republic, between the comfortable southerners after independence and the Irish in Northern Ireland who felt excluded. The 'border between people' divides families as well as communities and is more complex than sectarianism or disputes over the constitution. The rifts that run through the Irish people are far more extensive and complex than the one wriggly line that sets the boundary of states.

*

When I was five years old, my father got work in Belfast and we moved again, to another newly built house on an unfinished housing estate close to the remnants of a Second World War army camp with old Nissan huts, a grey water dam used for God knows what, and a mass of tangled barbed wire, which we, as small children, pressed down to make a path through into the fields. Growing up in Belfast, we were as far from the Irish border as from parts of Scotland, but right on top of another cultural border between Protestants and Catholics.

I grew up on a housing estate called Riverdale. Is there any other kind of a dale than one created by a river? An old map tells me the area was previously called Rivervale. What's the difference between a vale and a dale? Not much apparently. The renaming divided us from a past in which this land was open country.

There was a little river flowing near our house. Presumably sheep once grazed near it. It was really just a stream and came south between the rear gardens of streets that backed onto each other. The river appears not to have had a name that anyone remembered until it joined the Woodlands river near the dam. We would catch sticklebacks, or spricks, and keep them in murky water in jam jars until they died. My mother warned us against playing near the water in case we got polio. She was a nurse, so presumably she knew what she was talking about. There had been a recent outbreak, and a boy in my class at school wore callipers on his legs because polio had drained the strength from them. The stream was later designated the La Salle river, probably by water service workers to save them the trouble of poring over old maps to find out what it was really called.

There is nothing Irish about the name of Riverdale, though older names around us did have Irish origins and implications, like Finaghy Road, Bingnian Drive, Bearnagh Drive and Slieve Gallion Drive. Some streets around us had been named after Irish mountain peaks, while the later ones celebrated the Ulster aristocracy: Ladybrook, Stewartstown, Suffolk. Even streets in the city that remembered Donegal were named after lords and ladies who had added an L to their stature: Donegall Street, Donegall Square. The older streets off the Falls Road that led into the city retained names that marked old colonial ventures. There was Crimea Street and Cawnpore Street, which is what a plummy upper-class British accent had made of the Indian name Kanpur.

There was ongoing anglicisation by a city corporation which perhaps had not noticed that names like Belfast, Finaghy and Shankill were not English names at all. They were Irish words harshened by the Belfast accent to be satisfactorily chunky and earthy in the mouths of dockers and shipbuilders.

Belfast worked a similar chemistry on my own name, making Dockerty out of Dordy, as my father pronounced it. Even he hardly voiced the O prefix, making it more an 'Uh' than an 'O'. I only learned later that his father had not used the O at all, though all of his children did. Perhaps it was my Irish-speaking grandmother who had insisted on restoring it, if she thought the loss of it suggested that our forebears had had the good sense to 'take the soup' rather than starve, not a choice that would stand to their credit in a culture that honoured martyrdom. Neither the Irish themselves, nor their detractors, would claim pragmatism as one of their traditional virtues, and dying for your faith was what a decent Irish mother would expect of you if the occasion arose. At least the singing in the pews suggested as much.

'How sweet would be our children's fate, if they, like them, could die for thee.' That's from the hymn 'Faith of Our Fathers'. It's an English hymn honouring English martyrs, but we weren't to know that.

My mother pronounced our name, O'Doherty, as I have always done: O Daw Her Tae. She also insisted on calling my father Bernard, though everyone else called him Barney. Perhaps there was some class pretension at play there; another border which demanded that you locate yourself on one side of it or the other. Barney was more working class than Bernard, perhaps more Irish too.

As a child I bristled at the Belfast pronunciation of my name used all around me, though, in fact, that is closer to the actual Irish, Ó Dochartaigh. That 'ch' shouldn't be a full on 'k', more a hard 'h' from further back in the throat, but Belfast has never been known to soften a consonant. The hard 'h' was actually taken to be the hallmark of the Irish Catholic, the sound that would betray you and get you shot, the test question of later loyalist killers unsure of their target: 'Spell Harry.'

Around us in Riverdale, most of our neighbours were Catholics. Our local church was St Agnes's. Some of our neighbours were Protestants, most of them families of policemen who cycled every morning to the Royal Ulster Constabulary (RUC) station – or barracks, as we called it – at Dunmurry. We and the Protestant children went in different directions to school, our parents in different directions to work, even favouring separate bus routes, Catholics taking the red bus down the Falls Road into the centre of town, Protestants the green one down the Lisburn Road.

So the division in Ireland was not just a line on a map, which was more indistinct the further away you were from it. It was many divisions. My father and mother had different lineages, the one inclining my father towards basic republicanism, the other inclining my mother towards an empathy with things British. Not only had her mother grown up in England, but she had herself worked as a nurse in London through the Blitz. Presumably that's where she learned you could get polio from catching spricks. She did not have the reflexive wariness of the British soldier that I was to acquire later. She had probably dated soldiers. Her sister married a GI, who was himself a migrant from eastern Europe, and went off to Ohio. My father had also had his perspective widened by the war, where he worked among American troops stationed in Derry.

In our interactions with Protestants, my mother's concern was that their different way of life, different schools and churches, would tempt us into suspicion or derision. For her, what was more important than being friends with them was being civil towards them and never mentioning, for instance, the Easter Rising, for which there was that big commemoration when I was fifteen, or expounding on nationalist politics. She forbade me to fly the tricolour from an upstairs window. Few of our neighbours flew it either.

Mum was a part-time night nurse and she would come home with stories about the people she worked with who had 'seen the light' and trusted now that they were assured of a place in Heaven. It was as if she was bringing reports from a distant country about a people wholly unlike ourselves and beyond our comprehension. Once she was deeply upset by a patient who refused to have her near him because he said he saw the mark of the beast on her brow. She was still upset when she was telling us the story. I was surprised by her tears, but more curious about what the man had said than about why it had hurt her so. 'Did he really see something on your forehead?'

In most of her stories there were 'sensible Protestants' who were as appalled by the 'saved' as she was.

Another division that I was aware of was between me as an outsider and the local Belfast boys of my own age. I had started school in Ballycastle in a mixed 'babies' class where there were girls, nuns teaching us, and minimal corporal punishment. Instead of a cane, we were slapped on the palm of the hand for misdemeanours with a strip of light wood ripped from an orange box. The boys in Belfast seemed harsher to me. For some reason I was struck by how they said tagger instead of tiger, though we can't have had many conversations about beasts of the jungle. They fought and bragged about fighting. I was picked on as a boy in Belfast in a way I never had been before. Walking past a stranger he might say, 'What are you looking at?' This was a question to which there was no safe answer.

The all-boy classes concentrated their smells and their brashness.

When we moved to Belfast, rooms in the Casement Park GAA pavilion were used for our classes until a Catholic school could be built. The state was obliged to provide us with school places, but there was no consideration at all that we would take them. That would have involved taking a school bus out to Lisburn and sitting with the children of our Protestant neighbours.

In Casement Park we were slapped with proper canes shaped like walking sticks. There must have been a factory somewhere making them. I can still recall with ease the smell of that pavilion. It was a cocktail of cold damp cement, urine and sawdust.

The boys around me had their own pride in Belfast. On occasion a teacher would call one up to the front of the class to sing, and the song would often be 'The Belle of Belfast City'. It's a ballad about sexual harassment, which wasn't thought to be such a big deal at the time: 'I'll tell me ma when I go home, the boys won't leave the girls alone ...'

Even the republican tradition had local emphases. Through the songs and the stories of Belfast I heard relics of a republican culture which was urban and sectarian. A Belfast republican might wonder why the story of the city's experience up to then hardly featured in the popular paperback biographies of famous Irish Republican Army (IRA) men like Tom Barry and Ernie O'Malley, and feel that much of Belfast's story was sidelined. I was reading about Seán Treacy and Dan Breen and the Third Tipperary Brigade. Belfast's renowned Battle of Raglan Street didn't feature in any of the books I devoured when I was enthusing naively as a young lad about the IRA.

The concern of young people growing up in Belfast when I was young was not that they were cut off from places that were part of their patch, places within walking distance of their homes, though that would come later, with improvised barricades and formal peace lines. But even these wouldn't be much of a nuisance when areas homogenised themselves into wholly Protestant or wholly Catholic. Not many people would have to cross a peace line to get to the school of their choice.

Rather, our concern, in this industrial city, was that employment prospects would be hindered by Protestant bigotry. Though our parents would never have considered sending us to anything but a Catholic school, we knew that the school we'd name on a job application would define us as Catholic and nationalist, someone who did not respect the state, who had not been educated within the state system, who was learning God knows what from those religious orders.

A good example of this was my friend Frankie Callaghan, who got a job in the shipyard and stayed until the day another worker threw a knife into a board just inches from his ear and told him that his sort wasn't wanted there. He left and joined the British Army.

Fear of facing dangers like that would simplify the world. A young man would want to know where he was safe and where not. So he might easily adopt a mental map of a city split in two, corresponding with a larger map of an island split in two, and lose sight of a greater diversity.

2

WHAT ARE WE LIKE?

THE TRADITIONAL PRESUMPTION that Ireland could be one country included the idea that we were one people, that we have characteristics in common with each other. This is a quaint and obsolete idea in an age in which diversity demands respect, and differences in gender, sexuality and ethnicity are offered as more viable markers of identity than national origin. But it has been important in the past to assert Irishness as distinctive.

My aunt Peg's account of family history says that my grandparents in Plymouth, a hundred years ago, retained their sense of being Irish. I wonder how they did that. There was no radio or television then to bring Irish music or news into their homes, to connect them with the land to which they felt they belonged.

A devout Catholic, my grandmother's connection to other Irish people would have been mainly through the Church. She had, perhaps, little distinction in her mind between being Catholic and being Irish, though it was hardly the Latin Mass that provided the connection as much as the people around her in the pews. Then the priest's back was turned to the congregation. There was no Sign of Peace ceremony at which worshippers are invited to shake hands with those in the pews nearby. But there would still, no doubt, have been activities, including the confraternity and annual parades at Easter or Corpus Christi, when a girl would have dressed up and walked with her classmates and found social opportunity.

I imagine her to have been conservative, restrained and devout. For other Irish people there would have been the pubs and, where there were Irish clubs, the céilí and, at that time, political rallies and rebel songs.

How does one feel Irish? What did Peg mean by my grand-parents' 'sense of being Irish'? To the outsider and the nostalgic immigrant, the answer to that question may be simpler than for those at home.

The sensibilities of many Irish people on Twitter were affronted recently by a trailer for a film called *Wild Mountain Thyme*. The trailer played up to familiar, shallow cliches about the Irish: that we are romantic, pugnacious, not very bright and that we obsess about land; that our women have red hair; that our landscape is entirely rural. It was wonderfully parodied on Twitter by people who know that Ireland is not like that and who laugh at those who think it is.

Ireland has changed – not that it ever was like the world of *Wild Mountain Thyme*, but it was once content to be thought so. The tourist industry in Connemara still caters for those who think that *The Quiet Man* was a fair representation of Irish country life: that you could walk into any pub and the men at the bar would be singing and welcoming you to join them, and the way to tame your wife was to drag her home and kick her arse. If you were a real man she'd not hold that against you.

At home we are more sceptical of these sentimental and mythical notions of Irishness. Our actual country pubs can be dour and dark places, where no one spontaneously bursts into song and would get thrown out if they did.

We live in an era when all generalisations and stereotypes are frowned upon, and the momentum of that consideration presumably energised the disdain for *Wild Mountain Thyme*. But still, we like to think well of ourselves. We have our own cherished stereotypes. We have notions that we are fine decent people, though we don't call ourselves the land of saints and scholars anymore. Still, some of that pride in native decency and the notion that we are more heartfelt and poetic than others, particularly the English, still works in us.

We like it that outsiders think we are sensitive, mystical and unworldly. The novelist Jeffrey Archer, speaking on Radio Ulster's *Talkback* in October 2021, demonstrated how vivid the romantic casting of the Irish is still. His story went down well with the audience though it was entirely implausible. He said, 'I remember once in O'Connell Street. I was heading to Eason's to do a book-signing session in the middle of that wonderful road and I passed a tramp sitting in a corner who was reading the *Financial Times*. And only in Dublin could you find a tramp reading the *Financial Times*.' Unless perhaps he preferred *The New Yorker* or *The Economist*.

But there are no tramps any more. The tramp of earlier days was a wandering mendicant who lived on the road and slept under the stars. Perhaps there never was such a type and it was always a romanticisation of poverty and desperation.

Archer went on, 'And he looked up at me and he said, "Do you have any Irish blood in you, Jeffrey?" And I said, "Honestly I don't, at least not that I am aware of."

'He said, "It surprises me, because you are a *seanachie*."

'His wisdom has taught me to believe that I am a storyteller, not a writer.'

And this is a storyteller's story, founded on a cocktail of Irish stereotypes: the wise wanderer attuned to the ancient ways, no ordinary homeless derelict, but a sage who has survived into the modern world where he has to watch his share prices. Actually, it disproves its own assumption and demonstrates that an English man can be as much of a spoofer as any paddy.

But even more critically regarded writers have played with this idea of the more refined spiritual sensibility of the Irish. In Ian McEwan's novel *The Children Act*, a High Court judge called Fiona Maye visits a teenage boy in hospital to assess whether he is fit to make a decision to refuse a life-saving blood transfusion, in keeping with his Jehovah's Witness faith. She has been shielding her emotions for some months after a difficult case in which she had to determine that one conjoined twin should die to save the other, the alternative being to let both die.

When she is with the boy, at his bed, confronted by his implacable precocious reasoning, she allows something softer and more intuitive to work in her, to the clear disdain of her English companion. She invites the boy to play to her on his violin (a guitar in the film version) and corrects his fingering and sings along with him. And what does she sing? 'Down By the Salley Gardens', a Yeats poem put to music. The understated point here is that it is her romantic, intuitive, impulsive, compassionate Celtic nature, which has broken through.

The stereotype unfolded here is more lightly managed than in Jeffrey Archer's tale, but it is there. And it is not one that most Irish people would dislike. Most of us have little difficulty with the myth that we are humane, spiritual, creative and more besides, better than the English.

Even as Ireland has become more secular in recent decades, it has retained a sense that it is a spiritual country. We have a poet for a president. That is the Irish way. We are wholesome, warm-hearted, unmaterialistic people. We don't have nuclear power stations and when migrants are faced with deportation, their children's schoolfriends organise protests in support of them.

The presenter of the Friday night *Late Late Show*, Ryan Tubridy, often delivers a little homily to the audience about their support for charity and their diligence during the Covid lockdown, with the phrase 'this is who we are', reminding us that goodness is what defines Ireland. It is no longer about Catholicism and the foreign missions, but it is the same idea – that at heart we are generous, empathetic. That's in our Irish nature.

The Taoiseach, Micheál Martin, announcing tighter restrictions across the Republic to contain the coronavirus in the winter of 2020, spoke of those who had died when funerals and church services were limited, 'who didn't have the wakes and goodbyes we are so good at'. Death is one of the things we manage differently in Ireland, where the open coffin is set up in the living room so that the neighbours can come in for a last look at the deceased and then go to the kitchen for a sandwich and a cup of tea in the best china.

There are other versions of who we are that are much less complimentary, though there are some Irish jokes that are enjoyed by many in Ireland. For instance, at school in the 1950s and 1960s I knew lots of jokes about Paddy Englishman, Paddy

Irishman and Paddy Scotsman. If I remember rightly, Paddy Irishman was always more clever than the other two. Then there were the jokes about rabbis and priests which Dave Allen developed. Allen's jokes subverted the idea that the Irishman was simply stupid, a common theme for English comedians alongside mother-in-law jokes. He took us to the wake and into the confession box because he knew what happened in those places. This was an advance on the joke that asked: Did you hear about the Irishman who bought a pair of water-skis and went looking for a lake that sloped?

The sneering at the trailer for *Wild Mountain Thyme* was the most acerbic response I remember in Ireland to this easy stereotyping of the Irish. Modern Ireland does not want to be thought quaint, rustic and superstitious any more. Yet these qualities have been standard in the depiction of the country. Just as a filmmaker presenting a documentary on India will want to include a shot of a tiger, despite the tiger having no place at all in the lives of a billion people there, when it comes to shooting Ireland, directors want images of roadside grottos or Falls Road murals and women with red hair.

When Paul Merton on *Who Do You Think You Are?* was filmed driving from Waterford to Dublin, the car was shown weaving through narrow country roads. Actually, there is a motorway for the whole of the route, but that wouldn't look like the real Ireland of a film director's imagination.

The image of us as intuitive and poetic has its negative side. Our emotional natures are occasionally excessive. So we are also often depicted as irresponsible, drunken, fanatical and pugnacious. For example, Margaret Noble, an Irishwoman who became a Hindu nun and an Indian nationalist, is described by several of her biographers as having had a fiery Celtic temperament. What this means is that she was moody, perhaps that she suffered a volatility that today would be diagnosed as bi-polar disorder. But the example of Noble demonstrates that the notion of the Irish as emotionally extravagant had tempered even the understanding of educated Indians more than a hundred years ago.

There are two considerations here: how others portray us and how we would like to be portrayed, and one is perhaps as facile as the other. But both versions of us endure.

When being Irish means being part of a story driven by passion, and being characterised as naturally more sensitive, musical, eloquent and wronged than others, then it is an identity the romantic outsider might hope to have a share in. So most American presidents must have Irish roots and make a visit to the old homestead. Donald Trump, having no poetry in his soul, didn't make that essential pilgrimage, though he bought land in the west and built a golf course in Doonbeg, County Clare, which he probably doesn't know means Little Fort. He would probably prefer to be identified with a Big Fort.

The actor John Hurt thought that he would uncover his true Irish identity when he subjected his past to research for *Who Do You Think You Are?* The problem was that he didn't have any Irish roots and he conceded that the discovery was a huge disappointment. It took away from him a sense of who he was. This seemed unjust, because he had Irish traits – that wit, that wry humour, the rugged rustic looks and the hair.

Others have adopted an Irish identity and been accepted, like the English-born Micheál Mac Liammóir and Seán Mac

Stíofáin. Mac Liammóir founded the Gate Theatre in Dublin, Mac Stíofáin helped found the Provisional IRA. Both went to excess, taking on Gaelic names which are even more rare in Ireland than the red hair you'd have to have if you were to appear in a magazine ad for Irish whiskey, though Photoshop can fix that for you now.

It should actually be easy to pass yourself off as Irish, even with an English accent, because there are more Irish in England than there are in Ireland. But not everyone knows that, so a notion of Irish authenticity can plague the lives of Irish grandchildren coming home for the summer with their English and American accents.

But why should Ireland have distinctive characteristics? The main reason is that it justifies national independence from Britain. Our determination to distinguish ourselves from the British, impossible as that is, given how many of our cousins live in Britain now, includes not just a sense of historic grievance, but also a notion that we are a better people than they are.

One of the starkest examples of this idea is the Moving Hearts song, 'Irish Ways and Irish Laws', also recorded by Sinead O'Connor. One of its lines says, 'we are a river flowing'. The song declares that there is a pure Irish way of living that has been oppressed and contaminated, but which survives still and which will ultimately prevail.

When independence movements strengthened in India and Ireland at the start of the twentieth century, they made their separate cases for independence in similar ways. Margaret Noble in India and Patrick Pearse in Ireland put together similar arguments that their countries needed to assert native cultural and religious traditions as grounds for rejecting government by

Britain. Do we still have an indigenous Irish culture that must be preserved? Have we ever had one?

In the late nineteenth century, the Gaelic League was established to revive a lost culture centred on the Irish language and sports. Some followers of the League believed that an ancient Gaelic order had bequeathed to us ways of doing and thinking that were more natural to us. However, there were two big historic breaks in the transmission of this Gaelic culture down to us. One was the collapse of that order with the Flight of the Earls. The other was the Great Famine, which destroyed the peasant culture within which the language had been maintained.

The Gaelic Leaguers argued that we would not be true to ourselves and our Gaelic nature unless the earlier language and culture were revived. Yet some research suggests that the peasant Gaelic culture of the west at that time was not actually a remnant of an old order, but a response to the conditions of its own time. This idea is developed by Alf MacLochlainn in an essay 'Gael and Peasant' (Casey and Rhodes (eds), 1977). When Yeats and Lady Gregory and others sought to explore the Gaelic culture of the impoverished west, they did not find a link back to an ancient order but, instead, to the more recent and depleted pre-Famine Gaelic culture. For a time, around 1840, there were more Irish-speaking people in the country than before or since. They were the poor peasantry, the most vulnerable, the stratum of society that the Famine almost eradicated.

But it was the idea of the Irish language being a link back to a rich and ancient culture that stirred the Gaelic revival. One of the most prominent proponents of this revival, Patrick Pearse, believed strongly in the idea of a noble Gaelic spirit. In his tribute to O'Donovan Rossa, the Fenian, he said, 'To him the Gaelic ways were splendid and holy, worthy of all homage and all service; for the English he had a hatred that was tinctured with contempt. He looked upon them as an inferior race, morally and intellectually ...' ('O'Donovan Rossa: A Character Study', in Pearse, 1924.)

The Gaelic revival was predicated on an idea that we were intrinsically better than the English, who, in turn, thought they were better than us. It is perhaps not surprising that the Irish made such an assertion when we were so used to English derision, as when Punch described us as 'the missing link between the gorilla and the Negro'. (*Punch* 11, 1842, quoted by Lebow, 1977.)

Richard Ned Lebow is a distinguished American political scientist who has specialised in international relations and the causes of war but has taken a close interest in Ireland. He did his PhD thesis on British colonialism with the stark title 'White Britain and Black Ireland'. He has explored the anomaly that many in nineteenth-century Britain found contrasting explanations for poverty in England and in Ireland. The same authorities who campaigned for the industrial poor on the grounds that they could not be held responsible for the economic forces that denied them work, would blame Irish poverty on moral failings in the Irish character. That was their way of ridding themselves of a problem that was simply too big to be solved. (It has to be said, of course, that twentieth- and twenty-first-century British governments have had no difficulty in blaming the English unemployed for their own misfortunes.)

Lebow offers numerous quotes to illustrate this prejudice against the Irish. This one is from *The Times* at the very height of the Famine in 1847: 'What is an Englishman made for but work? What is an Irishman made for but to sit at his cabin-door, read [Daniel] O'Connell's speeches and abuse the English?' Also from *The Times*, on 6 January 1847: 'He is great at a hard bargain, still greater at a job when he supposes he has effectively "done" you' (quoted by Lebow, 1977). The Irish were seen as lazy and fickle, ready to undermine their own interests out of spite.

This was an enduring myth about the Irish, that they were congenitally inadequate. British Prime Minister William Pitt addressed the House of Commons on the problems presented by Ireland in 1799, on the very eve of the Union. He said the root of the Irish problem lay – 'in the present character, manners and habits of the inhabitants – in their want of intelligence, or in other words their ignorance … in the rancour which bigotry engenders and which superstition rears and cherishes' (quoted in Kee, 1980).

The preferred Irish stereotype contrasts with this – we are lavish, affable, poetic, spiritual and volatile, but fundamentally decent. And we don't just want to dismiss the negative stereotype, but to assert a positive one. The view that we are spiritual and creative is particularly attractive for being the opposite of our perception of the British: that they are legalistic, petty and class-bound.

It's unlikely that a book like Patrick Riddell's *The Irish: Are They Real?* (1972), with its simple unreserved racism, would be published today. But the question remains: if one cannot make generalisations about Irish characteristics or Irish culture, then who or what are we talking about when we use the word Irish? Is Ireland merely a civil polity circumscribed by territory, the sea and the emerging concerns of successive generations?

Some would tell us we owe a debt to history, an obligation to preserve tradition. Desmond Fennell argued that the Irish nation was founded on the narrative of 'liberationist nationalism' and that harm was done to modern Ireland by those who diminished or revised that story:

> Every nation in its here and now, the people who make up the nation now, have needs with respect to their national history. They need for their collective well-being an image of their national past which sustains and energises them personally, and which bonds them together by making their inherited nation seem a value worth adhering to and working for. (Fennell, 1989, p. 67.)

For Patrick Riddell, simplistic superficial cliches were sound assessments of Irish racial characteristics. We are a people who think of the law as a set of rough guidelines rather than clear rules. And we are so eloquent. We took the English language from the English and handed it back to them with a bit more dash and flare in it.

Most countries probably have notions of their own exceptional character and these tropes have all probably also got darker versions. Fintan O'Toole has ascribed the rise of English nationalism and the Brexit vote to a sense of English exceptionalism. The US declares itself openly to be the 'land of the free and the home of the brave'. But perhaps modern difficulties for both countries arise from the need to defend self-regard when its plausibility withers.

In which case, we might ask how Ireland, too, is to cope with the erosion of its foundation myths. Is Ireland a country or a state of mind? Perhaps it is natural for the people of a mass diaspora like Ireland's to look for characteristics in themselves that they can think of as distinctly Irish. They find a liking for poetry and declare they have Irish souls. What does Joe Biden mean when he says he is Irish? He means, at least, that he will take some responsibility for the old country's welfare because that is where his forebears lived. But he also seems to imply that there is something of the old country's ways in his character and his thinking.

The President of Ireland, Michael D. Higgins, has a word for Irish character. It is 'ethical'. I think the more likely word in my grannie's time in Plymouth and much later still would have been 'Catholic'. Higgins, I suspect, wants to get away from the Catholic designation but to retain the tradition that says we are innately good people.

Éamon de Valera had wanted to fashion an Ireland that was 'not only Catholic but Gaelic as well'. Higgins' use of the word 'ethical' marks the end of a time in which Ireland was defined by Church allegiance but retains within it the sense that we are a better people than others. In his inaugural speech in 2011, he said, 'Now is time to turn to an older wisdom that … many of the most valuable things in life cannot be measured by monetary success.' (Quoted in Higgins, 2017.)

Higgins was aware that the age of the Celtic Tiger had passed and had nearly resulted in economic ruin. It was time now

to close a chapter on that which has failed, that which was not the best version of ourselves as a people, and open a new chapter based on a different version of our Irishness

that will require a change in our political thinking, in our
view of the public world, in our institutions, and, most
difficult of all, in our consciousness.

We had lost our way, but we could find it again. The Irish
character was spiritual and unmaterialistic. This was close to
the version of Irishness favoured by de Valera: self-sufficient
and practical, but only in order to be freed for higher reflections,
beyond the reach of the rising filthy modern tide. But we had
just come through the bursting of an economic bubble; the
rogues had had their way, pursuing wealth built on chimeric
foundations.

Thomas Carlyle, writing in 1839, had a similar prescription
for our improvement but framed it within an acerbic rebuke:
'Immethodic, headlong, violent, mendacious: what can you
make of the wretched Irishman? … Such a people circulates not
order but disorder through every vein of it; – and the cure, if it
is to be a cure, must begin at the heart; not in his condition only
but in himself must the Patient be all changed. Poor Ireland.'
(Quoted in Deane, 2021, p. 104.)

Unlike Carlyle, Higgins says that the cure is at hand. Irishness comes in different expressions. One of them is avaricious
and soul-destroying, but there are other expressions that can be
reawakened in our consciousness, apparently with reference to
ancient wisdom. There is something in us as a people that the
world acknowledges and admires:

> Our successes, after all in the eyes of the world have been
> in the cultural and spiritual area – in our humanitarian,
> peace building and human rights work, in our literature,

art, drama and song, and in how that drama and song have helped us cope with adversity, soothed the very pain they describe so well, and opened the space for new possibilities.

It is an old idea that we are distinctly moral and spiritual. Daniel O'Connell, in a speech at Mullaghmast in September 1843, voiced better than anyone that Irish faith in their exceptional merit:

> Yes, among the nations of the earth, Ireland stands number one in the physical strength of her sons and in the beauty and purity of her daughters. Ireland, land of my forefathers, how my mind expands, and my spirit walks abroad in something of majesty, when I contemplate the high qualities, inestimable virtues, and true purity and piety and religious fidelity of the inhabitants of your green fields and productive mountains.

O'Connell was speaking before the Famine, practically on the eve of it, but still at a time when horrific poverty prevailed. There was little real dignity in Irish peasant life, where people were stuck in a poverty trap which denied them the incentive to improve their conditions lest their rents go up to absorb the cost and more. Alexis de Toqueville, who travelled round Ireland in 1835, before the Famine, described people living almost stupefied lives, yet later others looked back on that period as almost idyllic. Alexander Martin Sullivan said the Famine had depleted the morale of a contented people: 'Nine millions of a population living at best in a light-hearted and hopeful hand to mouth contentment … I doubt if the world ever saw so huge a demoralisation, so great a degradation, visited upon a once high spirited and sensitive people.' (Sullivan, 'New Ireland' (1887), in Deane, 1991, pp. 192–4.) He believed that one of the characteristics of the people, damaged by the Famine, was their innate generosity. 'Relief of destitution had always been regarded by the Irish as a sort of religious duty or fraternal succour. Poverty was a misfortune, not a crime.' (Deane, 1991, p. 195.)

The nineteenth-century Irish nationalist John Mitchel was very clear about his sense of the Irish being a superior people. 'Can you picture in your mind a race of white men reduced to this condition? White men! Yes of the highest and purest blood and breed of men. The very region I have described to you [Northwest Donegal] was once – before the British civilisation overtook us – the abode of the strongest and richest clans in Ireland.' (Mitchel, 'Jail Journal' (1854), in Deane, 1991, p. 181.)

Irish writer Seamus Deane thought that the perception that there is such a thing as a native Irish character really emerged after the French Revolution, first as part of a general British determination to be distinct from the French, as dependable people with an individuality that would be resistant to revolutionary ideas, and later as a specifically Irish determination to be unlike the English. There was also, as seems clear to Carlyle, an eagerness among the English and Scots to regard the Irish as unfit for self-government. This would justify the Union.

Deane noted that the very function of the Irish stereotype, whether advanced by the English or the Irish themselves, is to make clear that we Irish are different from them. In the Irish perception we, being different, are entitled not to be governed by England. In the English perception we were unfit to govern ourselves. Higgins cuts across both and says we thrived in England and we made that country what it is.

The attraction of the idea of a national Irish character, for the British, was that it allowed them to blame the Irish for the difficulties in the governing of Ireland. It could not be that Britain was an unreasonable and despotic power, so it had to be that the Irish were just difficult, bothersome and unreasonable. As the idea emerged in the nineteenth century that the real blight on the country was the parasitic landed gentry, some in England began to argue that it was the Irishness of those landlords that made them callous and selfish and destructive of their own interests, as if this immaturity was breathed in from the very air.

The attraction for the Irish was that the same idea of us as foolish dreamers could be spun positively to describe us as creative and imaginative, not obsessively legalistic or materialistic like the British. An example of how a single idea like this could be interpreted in different ways is found in the observations by Patrick Pearse and Winston Churchill that the Irish were continually at war.

In the Proclamation of the Irish Republic, which launched the Easter Rising of 1916, believed to have been largely written by Pearse, there is the statement, 'In every generation the Irish people have asserted their right to national freedom and sovereignty; six times during the past three hundred years they have asserted it in arms.' That's a huge misreading of history, not least in that it attributes small revolutionary movements like Robert Emmet's protest in 1803 to 'the Irish people', most of whom had no idea what Emmet was up to.

Then take Winston Churchill's statement about the perennial truculence of the Irish: 'But as the deluge [of the Great War] subsides and the waters fall short,' he said in 1922, 'we see the dreary steeples of Fermanagh and Tyrone emerging once again. The integrity of their quarrel is one of the few institutions that has been unaltered in the cataclysm which has swept the world.'

The lie in both these statements is that the concerns of the Irish never change, but the salient point for the argument here is that from one perspective that is to their credit and from another it is merely tedious.

Churchill's focus was, of course, on Northern Ireland, where there is another division across which notions of native characteristics simplify their separate rationales for acrimony.

3

WHO ARE WE, REALLY?

IN HIS POEM 'Valediction', Louis MacNeice berates the Ireland of the twentieth century for its cultural impoverishment. He has left us the best account of Protestant contempt for a depleted Ireland, characterised by 'indifference and sentimentality'. A magnificent poem, which started out in an earlier draft as a verse within his *Autumn Journal* written on the eve of the Second World War, it leaps off the page like passionate oratory, so compelling that its pace hides its own rhyme structure.

The poem references the iconic images of 'dolled-up virgins' and 'hammers playing in the shipyard', so it is the whole island he is dismissing. He sees it as unified in its introspective obsessions and self-regard. He accuses the whole country of 'imposture', which he must either take part in or renounce, so he renounces it.

Another great writer, Sean O'Faolain, saw Ireland as having been both impoverished and enriched by colonisation. When he lists the great men of Ireland – women escaped his notice – he includes the 'colonist and native' and says 'the blending of two cultures finally brought about an interesting and vital mentality', such as, presumably, had not been there before (O'Faolain, 1944, p. 14).

More passionately and later, Hubert Butler recalled the
decline of the Anglo-Irish in his essay 'Anglo-Irish Twilight',
first published in 1978 (see Butler, 1986). The essay opens
with reference to a National Museum exhibition on the landed
gentry, which, he says, represented 'the skeletal structure of a
civilisation outwardly as dead in Ireland as that of the Hapsburgs
in Bohemia'. So dead was that culture, he wrote, that no one
now steps forward to mark the achievements of 'the Grattans,
Floods, Edgeworths, Parnells, Plunketts and a thousand others,
who had built that Anglo-Irish civilisation'.

Butler attributes the decline of that 'civilisation' to the Act
of Union and the custom, thereafter, of sending 'the brightest
and the bravest to England', where they learned nothing of
Ireland. 'Waterloo may or may not have been won on the
playing fields of Eton, but Ireland was certainly lost there.' He
recalls a culture which had perhaps been disgraced by landlord
excesses, defeated by the Land League, had its property passed
over to tenants by the Land Acts and then had seen the relics
of its significance destroyed in the Civil War. There were 139
country houses destroyed in the fifteen months from January
1922, 'many of them treasure houses of great beauty, with fine
libraries, whose owners had shaped Irish history'. Ireland,
from this perspective, had sunk with its independence into a
wilful amnesia in which a heroic and brilliant contribution was
written out of history.

(I am writing this in the Butler room in the home of Tyrone
Guthrie, now the Tyrone Guthrie Centre at Annaghmakerrig,
bequeathed to the writers and artists of Ireland and beyond as
a residency in which they may work surrounded by Guthrie
family books and furniture and ornaments, in rooms adorned

by works of contemporary artists who have stayed here. So there is still something left of the Anglo-Irish input.)

The Irish are not a single people. When the Gaelic peasantry from which the O'Dohertys and O'Hallorans sprang were sulking in their hovels, the Anglo-Irish were producing great literature in the big houses our rent payments supported. Then, while Gaelic dignity was recovering, the Anglo-Irish culture was losing its nerve and wasting its energies.

The great exponent of this idea in the nineteenth century was the journalist Standish O'Grady, who rebuked the aristocracy for their ignorance and decline. 'Christ save us all! You read nothing, you know nothing. You are totally resourceless and stupid.' (Butler, 1986, p. 77.) O'Grady was calling them back to a sense of responsibility for Ireland and their own tradition. This is not a case that is often made today. The landlords are best remembered for the depredations and the grief that they inflicted on poor, poverty-trapped tenants.

If the Anglo-Irish had retained control of Ireland they would have preserved the country's place within the Union and taken it into the Second World War. The Northern Protestant Louis MacNeice was appalled at our neutrality then. However, O'Faolain spoke for the new independent Ireland and justified its abstention from the war by its need to 'work out its destiny as undisturbed as may be – a most natural desire when one realises that they have been waiting through several centuries for the opportunity'. He has little doubt that the Irish have a 'national genius' that they are now free to develop and thanks Britain for leaving them to get on with that even at its time of greatest need.

I would like to have seen MacNeice's face reading that.

O'Faolain attributes some generosity to Britain leaving

Ireland alone to reflect on identity and purpose while others were busy curtailing the Nazis. But the Irish people were not disengaged from Britain. Many fought in the war and after it they worked to rebuild British cities. In a creative reimagining of that relationship between Irish people and the British nation, President Higgins invited the Irish in Britain to take pride in their contribution to building the British nation. He sought to enrich the stereotype of the Irish by adding industry and affinity with Britain to their list of attributes. He said we need no longer assert Irishness as something distinct from and hostile to Britishness. Yet making such an assertion is usually where any claim to independence must start.

In 2014 Higgins visited the Irish community in Coventry. This was immediately following a reception for him by Queen Elizabeth. He said there, 'The story of Ireland in Britain has many dimensions, but as president of Ireland I am immensely proud to bear witness to your continuing centrality in our national identity.'

In effect, working in England did not make you less Irish but was a fundamental part of the Irish experience.

Higgins continued, 'it is a joy to note that there is virtually no aspect of British civic or political life that has not been enriched by contributions from the Irish community. That success is due in no small part to the determination and character of those who settled here in more difficult times.'

Higgins' portrait of the migrant Irish worker transforming England into a better version of itself is a reversal of the image popular in song and lore of the hard-drinking, hard-fighting Irish, those referred to as McAlpine's Fusiliers in the famous song of the same name, who built the roads and the railways and the suburbs of London and Manchester but squandered their wages on drink and gambling before retiring drunk to cold beds in bleak digs, only to start again the next day.

Unfortunately, when Higgins sought an example of a two-way flow of people and influences in a British migrant coming to Ireland, he settled for the poet Philip Larkin coming to Belfast to work in the library at Queen's University. It is doubtful that Larkin saw himself as a migrant when he was moving from one part of the UK to another. Nor, like the Irish who went to Coventry, had he been fleeing poverty for the chance to earn a living. He was actually getting away from a needy mother and from love affairs that had become too entangled (Sutherland, 2021). But Higgins perhaps didn't know that.

Like Higgins, Sean O'Faolain saw immigration and return to Ireland as enriching, and he was critical of those who thought the country would be better off secluding itself from the modern world, though he was all for staying out of the war. Some Irish republicans 'would like to turn the clock back and begin all over again, as if the entire process of historical fusion had never occurred, and could be obliterated' (O'Faolain, 1944, p. 14). He dismisses as 'Celtophilism' rather than Anglophobia the idea that Ireland can be rebuilt on the revival of the Gaelic language, Catholicism and the elimination of the English tongue.

So the conception of Irishness, the type of people that we are and ought to be, has changed over generations and has always been contested, yet always there has been a determination to define us, as much among those who despise us as those who love us.

*

In the North the division is between – well there you have a problem for a start. The Catholics and the Protestants?

Yet the dispute is not theological, though for some it has been. Some wanted a Catholic Ireland and some wanted a Protestant state. None but a few eccentrics argue for either now, though in my own lifetime some of the violence there was driven by the urgency that one religious vision should prevail.

Wallace Thompson, a long-time close adviser to the Democratic Unionist Party (DUP) is an evangelical Protestant and a devout monarchist. He is one of those whose sense of Britishness relies on the royal family being Protestant. He told me, 'If a Catholic ascended the throne, any remaining feelings of Britishness would be severely diluted. I'd still value the economic and financial benefits of the union, but I'd certainly be open to considering a new Ireland. Indeed, I think the debate should be happening within unionism now.'

Wallace may be an oddity. I have met and interviewed him, and I have interacted with him often on social media. I find no lack of intelligence in him and nothing abrasive. He simply lives with a world view that is remote to me.

Others say that their Britishness includes a reverence for the monarchy but does not depend on it. Wallace's view contrasts with that of Mervyn Gibson, General Secretary of the Orange Order. Mervyn invited me to Schomberg House for breakfast. He had a big fry, then took me round the museum there to show me relics of Protestant achievement. He said, 'It is important to me that the monarchy is Protestant. But if the monarchy became Roman Catholic, we would not cease to be British. I would still want to be part of the United Kingdom.'

There seems no immediate danger of a Catholic king ascending the throne, but he said, 'We have to think realistically about what could happen to the monarchy and to prepare ourselves for whatever is there. Our loyalty to the crown mightn't be as strong, but it still would not affect our British citizenship.'

The big question is whether unionism is ideological or essentially ethnic. For Wallace Thompson it is ideological, in that it relies on the Protestantism of whoever heads the House of Windsor. If a future king – and at least the next three scheduled monarchs are male – were to convert to Catholicism, that would be the end of the royal defence of the Reformation and he might then more comfortably redirect his allegiance to an Irish state. But he is an ethnic Ulster Protestant.

There are few if any nationalists and republicans now whose ideological conviction is linked to reverence for the papacy, which would be the obvious counter to Wallace Thompson's monarchism. Yet nearly all nationalists and republicans trace their families back to Catholic parents and grandparents and were educated in Catholic schools. These are the descendants of the native Gaels, or suppose themselves to be. Their sense of being native Irish is linked by historic coincidence to their religious tradition but is stronger than that tradition. For instance, alongside the decline of religion in Northern Ireland we have seen a growing interest in the Irish language. That sense of being Gaelic is perhaps supplanting the Catholic identity, at least for some. However, it is hardly conceivable that it could grow to the scale that Catholicism once had.

Nearly all unionists – or at least members of unionist parties – have similarly come from Protestant backgrounds. They are mainly descendants of those sent to Ireland during the historic plantations, who never lost the sense of being British.

The religious distinction between these groups, down through the centuries, reinforced the opposing national affiliations. In both traditions, religion, in terms of the actual sets of belief and practice, is losing its significance. Ironically, it survives more as labels of different national identities than as a descriptor of belief. A tired old joke in Northern Ireland is that you can be a Catholic or Protestant atheist.

So it is hard to speak with accuracy about Catholic and Protestant communities, other than by changing the meanings of those words, which is unfair to real Catholic and Protestant believers. And retaining labels which are losing their relevance clutters the argument.

In a recent academic paper for the journal *Irish Studies in International Affairs*, Professor Brendan O'Leary described Stephen Farry of the Alliance Party as 'a cultural Catholic'. That label spares O'Leary the difficulty of addressing the complications arising from secularisation, but it also denies Farry the right to be defined by the politics he most energetically asserts, which is that he is neither nationalist nor unionist. Farry himself says, 'I come from a Catholic background, but wouldn't see myself as a cultural Catholic. I have moved beyond the two communities paradigm, and indeed argue that things were never that simple.'

Although the term 'cultural Catholic' seems to mean something, it hardly means much more than that someone's parents were probably Catholic believers. I am a cultural Catholic in that I retain the memory of the doctrines, icons and rites that I was familiar with in a far distant childhood.

A young friend – also a cultural Catholic – once showed me a bracelet made up of images of Catholic saints: The Little Flower, Dominic Savio, Martin de Porres, the usual run. He had no idea who they were, but I was able to name them for him. They had not featured in his Catholic education, his Catholic culture. So one 'cultural Catholic' can have radically different cultural baggage from another. Which is all beside the point anyway. The term has no more meaning than the word 'taig'. It denies people the right to frame their identity for themselves out of their own experience. It helps preserve a way of discussing Northern Ireland in terms of its divisions even as those divisions wither.

Still, let's look at the traditional prejudices these separate, unnameable Irish- and British-identifying communities have held about each other.

Speaking broadly, and attributing this to no specific individual, the Irish-identifying in Northern Ireland have seen themselves, like the Irish on the rest of the island, as creative and witty, while they have regarded their British-identifying neighbours as overly literal and a bit stingy. One could bring religion into this and imagine that the Catholics of Northern Ireland are the mother's children, the mother being Mary. They are the indulged ones, encouraged to play and forgiven their sins, whatever they get up to. The Protestants are, by contrast, children of the Father, God Himself, who expects them to be industrious and true to their word and to keep the sabbath holy – which is what they did for much of my life, closing the pubs on a Sunday and even the children's playgrounds.

This strikes me as a metaphor that works, at least descriptively. To use it predictively would be sectarian.

A senior BBC official, once asked by schoolchildren why there were so few Protestant writers and musicians, said that Catholics were more inclined towards song and poetry, while Protestants were more practical and, to give them credit, 'did invent the tractor'. In fact, it is absurd to say that Protestants are less inclined to song and poetry than Catholics are, though there have been traditions arising out of prejudice and discrimination which directed Protestants into jobs in heavy industry and incentivised Catholics to go for higher education. All this is obsolete now.

There is a vivid representation of Catholic sectarianism in Brian Moore's novel *The Lonely Passion of Judith Hearne*, published in 1955. In it, Judith Hearne is struggling to preserve an air of respectability while getting poorer and resorting to spasms of heavy drinking. The book is largely set in a guest house or 'digs' owned by a Catholic woman, and much of the conversation among her guests illustrates how respectability centres on regular Mass-going, reverence for the priest and disdain for Protestants. Interestingly, even the returned American, Madden, goes to Mass, though he rapes a young Catholic serving girl. The only character with any decency in the story is Moira O'Neill, who invites Judith to visit her every Sunday and tries to help her as she falls apart.

Judith Hearne would be happier if she wasn't bound by a need to retain a facade of respectability, which includes viewing Protestants as other and detestable, not that she actually meets any in the story. Moore describes a Belfast in which the myth of native characteristics is conscientiously preserved. But it doesn't come easy to anybody to uphold a community's sense of rectitude.

I was baptised a Catholic twice, but both have worn off. The first was on the day of my birth. I was born alongside a twin brother in a bedroom in our little house in Muff. We were both very small. Family lore has it that my twin was not expected to survive into a second day but was blessed with St Anne's water and thereby restored to robust health. More than a year and a half passed before the more formal baptism in St Patrick's, a little country parish church at Iskaheen.

I received my full induction into the Church before the reforms of the Second Vatican Council. I made my first confession and first communion at St Agnes's church in Belfast in the 1950s and was confirmed there also and became a soldier of Christ. My mettle was tested by the bishop at the altar rails with a light tap of his knuckle on my chin. I eschewed the devil and all his works and, while I was at it, I swore off all alcoholic drink until I was twenty-five.

The devil has had nothing to fear from me since and I broke my temperance pledge ten years before it was due to expire.

My confirmation was around the same time that the fictional Judith Hearne was moving into her new digs in Camden Street, with a picture of the Sacred Heart on the mantelpiece and two bottles of whiskey in her case, making yet another effort to sustain herself as a respectable Catholic woman.

At this time the working-class areas of Belfast were as religious as any other part of Ireland. The local Catholic church was crammed during several Masses each Sunday morning, often with people kneeling on the steps outside to try to meet their obligation. It was a sin not to go to Mass, a mortal sin, I believe, a breach of one of the six commandments of the Church, and people took that seriously.

Most of my education was at the hands of the Irish Christian Brothers in Belfast, southern Irish men with country accents. They seemed foreign and strange to us boys and we must have been as strange to them, with accents from the Belfast streets. I suspect some of the Brothers were Judith Hearnes themselves, unhappily bundled together in a house called An Dunan (The Fort). They were celibates in black, with a collar that was only white in the upper half, to signal that they were not full clergy. They would come into the classroom dishevelled and frayed, the soles of their shoes worn thin as paper on one side, with their little battered cases for their books and nicotine-stained fingers. We knew nothing of the homes they had come from.

There is an Irish thing, or there was, where older people had extensive social maps in their heads. If you told your uncle you sat beside a boy called Donnelly he would say, 'Is his father a butcher or is that his granda? Wasn't there one of the girls went out on the foreign missions? I know the one now; they came from the other side of Dungannon. One joined the army and the other was a skitter, God forgive me.' But no one could do that with the Brothers, because our connections did not extend to Limerick or Galway or Cork. Perhaps if my grandfather had still been alive, he would have said, 'Gibbons? They were all a sorry lot.'

The border ran through our classrooms. We were northern and urban, they were southern and rural, unhappy men mostly, I think, given that one of our recurring apprehensions was about whether one teacher or another would be in a good mood.

The Brothers had contradictory responsibilities. One was to make us as Irish as they could. The other was to make us fit, through education, for minor clerical jobs in the Northern Irish civil service or the Post Office. It was even considered possible that some of us might turn out fit for higher achievement and become Brothers ourselves or lay teachers.

Those rash enough to declare they had vocations to be Brothers were sent off at fourteen to the seminary at Baldoyle in Dublin. Those who wanted to teach would later make it into St Joseph's Training College in Belfast or to a similar college in Manchester. One didn't need A-Levels to train to be a teacher then, or a full degree to qualify afterwards. Teaching was, I think, regarded as about the best that the brightest of us would manage, a career to settle for when no one expected you would ever make it as a solicitor or a doctor.

The mission of the Brothers to Gaelicise us was pursued through language, sport and the céilí. Every boy took Irish up to the age of fifteen or sixteen. In the mid-1960s, when I was at school, the school leaving age was extended to sixteen, at which age we would sit the General Certificate of Education at Ordinary Level.

I liked Irish. I went to the Gaeltacht in northwest Donegal for a three-and-a-half-week immersion course where the teacher shouted at us constantly because, it being a holiday, he could not cane us. But the Brothers were not as successful at inculcating in us an interest in our lost native tongue as later cultural revival groups have been. During and after the Troubles many felt that they should learn and speak Irish to assert their identity as Irish people, having a stronger sense than previous generations that it had been robbed from them by our British colonisers. So, there is far more Irish spoken around Belfast now than there was then.

The Brothers organised Gaelic games, football and hurling, and in the schoolyard at lunchtime we often had our own
games of handball. Playing rugby or soccer would have been
unthinkable then. One Brother who learned that boys in two
classes had arranged a five-a-side soccer game in the gym
ordered all those boys who had played or attended to leave
his class and didn't let them back for two weeks. I saw him
at the classroom window watching boys playing with a ball
in the yard to check that they picked it up and didn't just use
their feet.

From the age of just thirteen, the Brothers had us dancing
with girls at céilís. Yet in religion class they were as emphatic
as any puritan in their condemnation of sins of the flesh. One
teacher used an American handbook which itemised at which
stages in a relationship with a girl it might be acceptable to
move from light kissing to heavy petting, and how to be on
the alert against what the book called 'the sexual urge'. Wet
dreams or 'nocturnal emissions' were a particular hazard. We
were assured that it was no sin to become aroused in sleep but
warned that if we woke up in such a state of arousal and helped
it along, that was a sin.

Still, the same Brothers marshalled us through the 'Waves
of Tory' in the Ard Scoil or the church hall at St Therese's, told
us when to take her hand, when to let go and when to get a
good hold of her and swing her round and not to let her slip
from sweaty palms. And the girls who came from the all-girls'
schools run by the Dominicans and other orders of nuns were
the first girls we all kissed, petted heavily and dreamed about.

We had the Brothers to thank for such opportunities and
this was presumably because making us Irish took precedence

over making us pure and saving us from Hell, which we all believed in then.

*

There are four basic levels of characterisation to be considered in the North: how Protestants see themselves, how they see Catholics, how Catholics see themselves and how Catholics see Protestants. All four, of course, are superficial stereotypes and generalisations of no practical application.

There are a few old cliches about Protestants. One is that they 'dig with the other foot'. Few will risk being specific about which foot that is. This may have come from some different types of spade used by the native Irish and by the Planters. I doubt it was ever meant as a precise way of labelling Protestants. It was more a kind of a code for sectarianism. Instead of saying bluntly that you suspected a man was a Protestant or a Catholic, you might say, 'he digs with the other foot'.

Once at the end of a wedding party in County Tyrone, the father of the bride approached me with a question. He knew me as someone who wrote about political and cultural affairs. He wanted to know if anyone had ever done clear research on the question of whether this difference between Protestants and Catholics was real; did our lot have a stronger leg on one side and they put their weight on the other?

What surprised me about this was that the man was not joking. He was hoping that someone had clear evidence of a physical difference between his people and 'the other sort'. He was well beyond thinking that the differences were merely of constitutional preference or religious belief, and he would not be easily brought to that position. He lived in a part of Tyrone which still retains a sense of their Protestant neighbours being alien and not yet fully belonging after only being about the place for 400 years.

A priest once explained Tyrone sectarianism to me. He said the ancestors of these people were put off their land during the Elizabethan Plantation, after the collapse of the old Gaelic order. They were driven to the bog and the hill, and they still see that the Protestant farmers have better land and regard that as having been stolen from themselves.

Most Northern Protestants see themselves primarily as British. They see their Britishness as being in some jeopardy, as indeed it is, because Northern Ireland is not as secure in the Union as Yorkshire is. A majority can vote the region into a united Ireland, assuming that the rest of Ireland agrees. This principle is enshrined in the Good Friday Agreement of 1998. As far as Northern Ireland is concerned, the Union is like an open marriage. London says, you can stay as long as you like, we love you dearly, but you know where the door is. But when Scotland thinks of leaving, England howls in anguish, pleads and threatens, and offers more freedom inside the Union.

So the terms on which Northern Ireland is accommodated are different. Scotland is like the cherished partner who hankers for the highway but is really wanted at home. Northern Ireland is like the surly teenager who is getting up the nerve to move out and suspects his parents will be glad to see the back of him. When England was voting for Brexit and discovered that Northern Ireland was going to be a complication, the reaction was like that of a rattled parent who had already assumed proprietary rights in the home. Are you still here?

It is a common mistake to think of the Protestant community as homogenous. There is a huge diversity of attitudes on social morality and culture, yet the big thing for most is the Union. Attachment to the Union in Northern Ireland extends from liberal secular-minded people who would never apply the term Protestant to themselves and might easily reconcile themselves to being Irish, to ardent, saved evangelicals who would die to resist unification.

Those Protestants who actually believe in the teachings of their Churches, are different from Catholics. Catholics are often recognised by their names, drawn from patron saints canonised by their Church. Protestants haven't had named saints since the Reformation and they don't traditionally insist on a first name being a 'christian name'. Often a child will be given a surname from the extended family, so we have, for instance, a Methodist minister called Johnson McMaster. We are also seeing in this generation a greater number of Gaelic first names, such as Saoirse and Firinne, along with the traditional Sinéads and Kevins, but these are almost exclusively among Catholics.

Protestants are sometimes credited with a different way of thinking, drawn from their faith in the Bible and their rejection of icons. Catholics believe that good works and charitable giving are likely to help them get into Heaven when they die, but much of Protestantism rejects this entirely, arguing that salvation is by faith alone. Calvinists reject even that and teach that only the pre-ordained elect get through. It has been argued that Protestants are more literal-minded, Catholics more intuitive. All nonsense of course. Yet within the Protestant culture there is a respect for a rejection of science and the theory of evolution because it contradicts the Biblical narrative of Creation.

Edwin Poots, a former first minister in Northern Ireland, believes that the world is 6,000 years old because the Bible says so, or he thinks it does. In fact it was Bishop James Ussher who came up with this figure in the seventeenth century, by tracing the chronology of events in the Bible back to a date of Creation.

In 2020 when Edwin was, for a brief spell, leader of the DUP, he visited an observatory in the Sperrins, and one has to wonder what he thought he was looking at, for if Creation was 6,000 years ago there can be nothing in the sky more than 6,000 light years away. Or maybe he thinks the speed of light is greater than what the textbooks say. The Bible isn't clear on the question.

Unlike Protestants, religious Catholics believe that revelation continues, often in the form of apparitions by the Virgin Mary. I explored this as a religious affairs journalist in the 1980s and discovered that she had been popping up all over the place.

Protestantism arose out of a revolt against the Catholic Church and a demand that Christians be free to read the Bible for themselves and make their own personal relationships with God. Fine. A great idea.

But from that follows an ongoing fear that Catholics do not think for themselves but are manipulated by their Church. This is not based on everyday observation so much as on the foundational inspiration of the Reformation. That Catholicism continued to have a hold on the lives of believers for further centuries has only reinforced that original vision. Further, some Protestant traditions would have it that all Catholics are doomed to burn in Hell. Paradoxically, some of the nicest people you could meet hold that private opinion about you, but they don't usually rub it in. Today there is no reciprocal teaching in Catholicism that all Protestants are damned, though many individual Catholics may privately believe it.

Many Protestants also feel that Catholics don't respect the state and the law as much as they should. These people lived through the Troubles preserving secrets from their Catholic neighbours for fear that information might get back to the IRA through them. So they would not divulge, even to a friend, for instance, that a brother was a police officer or a soldier. They are genuinely appalled that decent, good-natured Catholic neighbours regard the IRA campaign as having been an unfortunate necessity and vote for Sinn Féin.

Northern Catholics tend to think of themselves as survivors of oppression. This can manifest as confidence or as hurt. They were deserted by the South and subjected to discrimination by the unionists, but they can overplay the history of subjugation. My generation in its youth was better off in Northern Ireland than it would have been in the republic. My parents left Donegal in the 1950s for the benefits of good housing, a health service and welfare payments. The fact that demands for an end to discrimination against Catholics formed a legitimate motive for the civil-rights movement in the 1960s does not erase the simple fact that many, like my parents, were not discriminated against.

In my generation, the aspect of Catholic religious practice which would most have bewildered Protestants was the sacrament of Confession. Sins could be erased from the record. The Protestant coming before St Peter would be presented with a whole book full of transgressions. The Catholic who had managed to confess and receive absolution would be met with a blank sheet and a warm welcoming smile or, at worst, a limited period of burning in Purgatory. And the fact that we didn't live tormented by anxiety about Purgatory suggests we didn't really believe in it.

Protestants had rebelled against indulgences granted by Rome. These allowed time off or parole from Purgatory. Partial and plenary indulgences were still being cited as rewards for many devotional practices in my youth. Inevitably, Protestants who saw nothing in the Bible to support this get-out-of-Hell-free clause for Catholics saw it as evidence of their innate inability to comprehend the rules and respect the law. It is part of why we are so irresponsible. Others are irresponsible for different reasons.

Catholics, if I may generalise a bit, still see Protestants in some measure as people who presume to have authority over them and who don't really believe in equality. Obviously, this could never be said of all Protestants, other than by someone like that Tyrone man who believed that your faith expressed itself in the power of your right or left leg, not being sure which.

And perhaps neither community at heart fully regards the other as its equal. Each may even see itself as the essence of its proclaimed identity, the northern Protestant more British than the British, the northern Catholic more Irish than the Irish in the South.

Britain retains a Protestant monarch. If the rest of Britain is losing all sense of how vital this is to the country's identity, then at least the Orangeman holds fast to the sanctity of that tradition knowing that he is right and they are wrong.

The northern Catholic, through Sinn Féin, calls the South back to its waning commitment to a united Ireland. But northern nationalism's assumption that it can fit into a new

Ireland comfortably alongside what currently constitutes the Republic is questionable. In seeking to represent the essence of what it is to be Irish, it recreates an Ireland of the 1950s. The Church is not part of republican ethos any more, but the flag waving, the celebration of the IRA and the passion for the Irish language are all anachronistic in the eyes of the modern Dubliner.

A major task before a happy unification must be conciliation of the nationalist and unionist communities in Northern Ireland. What has been given less consideration is if or how northern nationalists can become more like Irish people south of the border.

The people most ardently for or against a united Ireland are the ones likely to have greatest difficulty adjusting to it if it happens. The people most likely to be at ease with it are the people who seem to care least, though even among unionists there are those who have long familiarity with an all-Ireland context: rugby players, presbyterian moderators, bishops of the Church of Ireland. Sinn Féin advances its cause in the South by working on issues of real concern to people there, housing and welfare. And that is a great strategy for garnering support there; but what is it doing to persuade people of the value of its core concern, the unification of Ireland?

*

In Ireland we have emerged from denial.

Catholic Ireland is dead and gone and good riddance. The nation used to define itself as Catholic and Gaelic, and while these definers were important to us for most of a century, we have now put them aside, if not yet wholly behind us. Within our presumption of Irish holiness and moral worth, or under its cover, there was much ignorance and cruelty towards the pregnant, the gay, the unhappily married, lovers who might have come closer together if they had not been taught that their very natures were sinful. Very quickly we unlearned those things, legalising contraception, divorce, homosexuality and abortion in a single generation. Earlier we had shed another denial, one that said we could live high and dry above the filthy modern tide, self-sufficient.

The Ireland imagined by Pearse and de Valera was progressively dismantled as unworkable. They envisaged a time when we would all speak Irish, stay on the island and live productive agricultural lives, with the men working the land and the women at home minding the children. Instead, we got the further ascendancy of English, as more Irish writers distinguished themselves with that supposedly foreign tongue and as successive generations became more alienated from Irish by the demand that they learn it in school. We exported more people than products and we welcomed the world's influence through British and American television.

In time we opened our economy to outside investment and the real drivers of cultural change turned out not to be surly chauvinistic men in tight suits or the clergy but role-model celebrities, and the prospect of freedom was opened up by new ideas like Women's Liberation and the secular conscience.

The generation that reached its teens in the 1960s brought a wave of Church dropouts, and as they grew older and had children, they told them that they didn't have to bother with that stuff. Church attendance plummeted and the religious orders practically died out. By 1980 no one in their right mind wanted to be a Christian Brother or a sister, and some orders actually had applicants subjected to psychological testing to explore their motivations.

The numbers going to Mass today, however, suggest a culture in which Catholicism is still important, even if the numbers signing up for the priesthood and the religious orders show that the commitment to the Church is not deep enough to warrant any young people making a career of it.

The children of that 1960s generation grew up to demand access to contraception, the legalisation of homosexuality, divorce, same sex marriage and abortion. They demanded employment and property rights for women. No more of the nonsense of a man having to vouch for them when taking out a bank loan, or their having to leave work on marriage. Some of them still went to Mass occasionally, got married in church and buried their parents with a priest in attendance, but they didn't go to Confession let alone into seminaries.

Curiously, when they did find themselves at Mass, for a funeral or a wedding or a nephew's confirmation, they would go to communion. Why? Because – well God knows why. Perhaps because it was less embarrassing than sitting in the pew on your own. Serious atheists wouldn't of course, but these weren't serious enough about religion to be conscientious believers in either God's existence or His non-existence.

The nation-building notions of Pearse and de Valera and their type were founded on denial. The presumption that we were religious at heart was founded on a denial of human nature. They understood of course that people lost their faith when they went to England for work but thought they could shore up a Catholic culture against English and international influence.

That fear that the emigrant would lose the faith goes back to the beginning of emigration, the heart of it being the sense that no other country was as pure and decent as Ireland. Daniel O'Connell, in his day, excoriating the Irish-Americans who defended slavery, wrote, 'It was not in Ireland that you learned this cruelty. Your mothers were gentle, kind and humane.' (Quoted in Ignatiev, 2009, p. 35.)

And when I was young and went to the Lenten Mission, the Redemptorists would scowl at us from the pulpit about the moral danger of going to work in England and the need to say the rosary every day or rely on a mother's prayers. A city like London, where people didn't even know their next-door neighbour, was a heartless and sinful place where many a good Irish girl had been led astray, where many an Irish man that was raised in a holy family had got drunk and gone off with a woman who had already fallen into sin and offered him comfort while dragging him closer to Hell.

Even in our denial of nature we were denying England, and the offer from the Church and chauvinistic nationalism was that we could be better than England, live more wholesome lives and save our souls too.

4

PADDY WAS THERE TOO

THE ASSUMPTION OF the Irish revolution is that an oppressed people shook off the shackles of imperial conquest and found a freedom to be themselves and to govern themselves according to their native genius.

For a hundred years, all of our history has been distorted when viewed through the lens of national struggle and the notion of a Catholic inheritance from ancient times. In consequence we have become blind to huge dramatic events in our past. The great dramas, like the rebellion of 1798 or the Famine, often had their sequels in foreign countries and these are little considered in histories of Ireland. The second chapter of the account of the rising of the United Irishmen is surely the role played by soldiers who fled after their defeat to Europe and fought for Napoleon. When Wellington confronted them at Waterloo, a huge part of his own army was Irish and thousands of them died on that cramped battlefield. Men on both sides had developed their military skills in Antrim and Belfast. How can that not be a bigger part of our story than the trifling and bizarre antics of Robert Emmet in 1803?

The second volume of the story of the Famine in the 1840s is surely the American Civil War of 1861–65, with huge numbers of Irish soldiers fighting and dying on both sides. And following from that came the formation of the Fenians and their attempt to invade Canada and trade it with the British for Ireland. That was as ambitious an endeavour as shooting up O'Connell Street in 1916.

It mattered at home what Irish people had done abroad. Even a history confined to events and experiences on the island alone should include the impact of events far away. There was money sent home by soldiering sons, and grief in Irish homes when those sons died in foreign wars. But all that carnage and grief was irrelevant to the writers of the Proclamation because it raised questions about how central Irish freedom was to general Irish concerns.

How Irish were we, after all, before the Easter Rising?

Certainly being Irish was different from being British and both nations knew that. But the Irish have created a myth that we have shuffled our way out of the grasp of the beast who attempted to devour us and we have ignored the part we played in the Empire. We were part of the British project. Under the terms of the Union we were not a colony, not as India was to be a colony, even if we were disparaged and abused and regarded as dangerous.

The most powerful story of our abuse at the hands of England is the potato famine of the 1840s, when government commitment to *laissez-faire* economics – leaving it to the market to find its own balance – expressed itself in the horrific notion that the Irish peasantry might starve or, out of hunger, discover sufficient entrepreneurial spirit to save themselves. The terms on which the government responded to this famine were much the same in Ireland as in the Highlands of Scotland: leaving market forces to find the balance.

In 1835, Alexis de Toqueville discovered the Irish peasantry living in appalling conditions which he and many of his interviewees blamed on absentee landlords and a system of tenancy which allowed them to raise rents as improvements were made to land and holdings. This was the ultimate poverty trap. Try to lift yourself up and you could end up worse off. Better then to live as many did at the most basic level, barely subsisting, in cabins that, said de Toqueville, might have been comparable to those of the Iroquois if they had had a hole in the roof to let the smoke out, where the pig living with the family had acquired the playful nature of a family pet, while the stupefied adults sat stunned and oblivious. And these same people were obliged to pay a tithe to the established Church though they were not part of it. There appeared strong grounds for revolution if the people had the energy for it, but the route out of squalor for many was enlisting with the British Army or the East India Company and becoming the Empire's enforcers abroad.

Previously, the discovery of great fighting men among the Irish had been forestalled by the Penal Laws. In the early eighteenth century, Catholics in Ireland were barred from the army and from owning guns. Thomas Bartlett says that this rule was first relaxed by the East India Company and that a 'blind eye was turned to the ban on Irish Catholic soldiers and there was an inevitable build-up in recruits from Ireland' (Bartlett, 1997). He traces the start of this to the 1750s and the Seven Years War.

The old folksong 'Arthur McBride' describes the efforts of British recruiting sergeants in Ireland at the time of

the Napoleonic wars. This isn't a rebel song. The singer
and McBride actually visit the sergeant to sound out their
options. (This differs from the better-known Paul Brady
version, in which they encounter him by chance on Christmas
morning.)

> and then after restin' we both took a tram
> to meet Sergeant Harper and Corporal Cram
> beside the wee drummer who beat up the camp
> with his rowdy dow dow in the mornin'

The Irish men cut up rough when the sergeant takes offence at
their spurning his offer of a guinea and a crown 'to drink the
King's health':

> Had we been such a fool as to take the advance
> with a wee bit of money we'd have to run chance
> 'Do you think it no scruples to send us to France
> where we should be killed in the morning?'

> He said, 'Me young fellows if I hear but one word
> I instantly now will out with my sword
> and into your bodies as strength will support
> So now me gay devils take warnin!'

These brave Irishmen can do without the guinea and the crown
and have little to learn about fighting from the army:

> But Arthur and I we both took the odds
> and we gave them no chance for to launch out their swords

our whackin' shillelaghs came over their heads
and we paid them right smart in the morning.

It is not surprising that by the time of the Napoleonic wars, when British regiments were keen to recruit Irish soldiers, their efforts were rewarded. Dan Harvey writes, 'Recruiting parties found thousands of fit and tough young men only too eager to embrace the military life and escape the arduous living conditions and the problems caused by the lack of education, opportunity and employment in an increasing population.' (Harvey, 2017, p. 12.) His account of the role played by Irish soldiers on both sides at the Battle of Waterloo says that the rush to recruit Irish soldiers started after the Catholic Relief Acts of 1778 and 1782 (Harvey, 2017, p. 11).

In a search of a British forces database, I found twelve Dohertys who fought in the Napoleonic wars, one of whom was a lieutenant colonel and one an assistant surgeon, presumably the guy that would have sawn off the remains of your blasted leg. Napoleon himself was confronted by a Lieutenant Theophilus O'Halloran.

Harvey includes the Anglo-Irish Duke of Wellington, who led the armies against Napoleon, among the Irish who fought at Waterloo. An *Irish Times* article marking the anniversary in 2015 rejected this. Ronan McGreevy wrote:

> Wellington was Irish in so far as he was born in Ireland and spent his youth in Ireland, but he was really a British aristocrat and imperialist. His allegiances were to his own class and to the British monarchy. He never self-identified as Irish though his family had been in Ireland

for centuries. It would not have occurred to him. (*The Irish Times*, 18 June 2015.)

I have a problem with saying that Wellington was not Irish, at least when it is said retrospectively. This is part of the denial of a past in which we were organically linked to Britain. O'Faolain, who saw Ireland as a merging of two streams, the Gaelic and the Anglo-Irish, would not have dismissed Wellington as essentially a foreigner. If Ireland is ever to be one country, it must incorporate its British history. The Battle of Waterloo was a major event in Irish history because thousands of Irish soldiers fought and died on both sides that day. If Wellington's Irishness is qualified by allegiance, so is theirs.

Wellington was not a Catholic or a republican or a nationalist, but to say that he was not Irish is to suggest that there is a more precise qualification for being Irish than having been born on the island. It is also to exclude the other Anglo-Irish whom Ireland might more readily want to be proud of, such as Jonathan Swift, Maria Edgeworth, George Bernard Shaw, Oscar Wilde, W.B. Yeats, Maud Gonne and Hubert Butler.

Wellington was a unionist. A future united Ireland which valued that tradition would have to recognise him as an Irish hero.

Daniel O'Connell, the Liberator, who sought the repeal of the Union, was determined to remind Britain of the Irish contribution to her military successes:

No man is ever a good soldier but the man who goes into the battle determined to conquer or not come back from the battle-field. No other principle makes a good soldier; conquer or die is the battle-cry for the good soldier; conquer or die is his only security. The Duke of Wellington had troops at Waterloo that had learned that word, and there were Irish troops among them. You all remember the verses made by poor Shan Van Vocht:

'At famed Waterloo
Duke Wellington would look blue,
If Paddy was not there too,
Says the Shan Van Vocht.'

Yes, the glory he got there was bought by the blood of the English, Irish, and Scotch soldiers –the glory was yours. (Speech at Mullaghmast, September 1843.)

This isn't a description of the sullen mercenary who goes to war for no other reason than to escape poverty, but an idealised account of men who would not even seek to escape death on the battlefield. Of course it was high-flown nonsense, but that's beside the point. It was addressed to an audience which was expected to find that nonsense exhilarating, who believed that the Irish at Waterloo were heroes of which they could be proud.

O'Connell was scathing and vigorous in his attack on Wellington and the government. He argued that the Union was illegal because the Irish Parliament had not had the authority to make constitutional change. But he professed that the people were loyal to the monarchy and claimed that a speech by Queen Victoria accusing the Irish of disaffection had been written by ministers and was not reflective of her own thinking:

> They put a speech abusing the Irish into the Queen's mouth. They accused us of disaffection, but they lied; it is their speech; there is no disaffection in Ireland. We were loyal to the sovereigns of Great Britain, even when they were our enemies; we were loyal to George III, even when he betrayed us; we were loyal to George IV when he blubbered and cried when we forced him to emancipate us; we were loyal to old Billy, though his minister put into his mouth a base, bloody, and intolerant speech against Ireland; and we are loyal to the Queen, no matter what our enemies may say to the contrary. It is not the Queen's speech, and I pronounce it to be a lie.

O'Connell had a style of oratory that reminds me of the Rev. Ian Paisley's, not just in its respect for the monarchy, but in its rural humour. Of course, he may only have been deferring to the monarchy to evade a possible charge of treason or sedition:

> This is our land, and we must have it. We will be obedient to the Queen, joined to England by the golden link of the Crown, but we must have our own Parliament, our own bench, our own magistrates, and we will give some of the shoneens who now occupy the bench leave to retire, such as those lately appointed by Sugden [the last English Chancellor of Ireland]. He is a pretty boy, sent here from England; but I ask: Did you ever hear such a name as he has got? I remember, in Wexford, a man told me he had

a pig at home which he was so fond of that he would call
it Sugden.

The Irish were poor, but armies valued them for their height.
Although they lived grim impoverished lives sustained by the
potato, it was nutritious enough to build them up taller than
the average English city worker and make Irish men more
attractive recruits.

Stereotypes influenced that judgement too. Bartlett says
that Irish soldiers were regarded as more enduring and
cheerful, better able to face adversity, having presumably been
accustomed to hunger and discomfort in the home cabins they
shared with hordes of siblings and the family pig.

We get a contemporary account of the recruitment of
soldiers in Ireland from *The Adventures of a Soldier*, published
originally in 1841 and republished in 2005 as *Rifleman Costello*
(Costello, 2005). Ned Costello, who was born in Mount Mellick,
Queen's County in 1788, got excited about the idea of joining
the army when he worked alongside an old soldier in his uncle's
shoe-making business and said he became 'red hot' for a soldier's
life. He joined the Dublin Militia at the age of eighteen. The
following year, while stationed in Londonderry, he volunteered
for the 95th (Rifle) Regiment. For that he was paid a bounty of
eighteen guineas, but had to pay £4, presumably to buy himself
out of the militia.

He then went to Dublin, where he was made part of a
recruiting party, the very type described in the song, who went
round trying to persuade fit young men to accept payment
and join up: 'I must say I felt highly delighted with the smart
appearance of the men, as well as with their green uniform.'

Poor Ned blew his allowance of a shilling a day and was soon hungry, broke, dejected and in serious need of recruiting someone for the £2 he would get. When a man approached him and offered to sign up if Ned would give him a shilling, he went into a pub, explained his problem to the landlord, borrowed a shilling and gave it to the recruit. The new man then spent the shilling in the pub, drinking with Ned until the sergeant arrived with the papers and the money.

Missing from the story is any suggestion of idealism on the part of Ned or the man he signed up, or indeed any qualms arising from being Irish or feeling that the war in France had nothing to do with him. The story also provides a sharp contrast with the ways in which men were shanghaied into the navy. Ned and his new friend jumped ship in Liverpool one night and dossed in a cellar after a night's drinking. There they were confronted when they awoke by men with cutlasses and bull dogs. Fortunately, they were able to send for their sergeant, who claimed them back for the army.

Irish aspirants to army life were said to prefer joining the East India Company to the regular army because the pay was better and there was the prospect of booty. Bartlett observes that the type of Irish soldier who joined the East India Company was the sort that would later be drawn to the French Foreign Legion, 'adventurers, rogues and petty criminals'. For the aristocratic Irish, the landed Protestants, joining the East India Company's army was seen as a shortcut to the prestige of an officer's life, with the added bonus of not having to pay for a commission, which they would have had to do in the regular army until the system was abolished in 1871.

When the East India Company first sought to recruit Irish

peasants for its army, the Lord Lieutenant, Lord Townshend, said he thought it a good idea because 'multitudes of tall, able-bodied men' were 'living most miserably'. Some were joining the armies of France and Spain, and Britain was losing the advantage of their 'military inclinations' (quoted in Bartlett, 1997, p. 14). By 1813, there were East India Company recruiting offices in Belfast, Dublin, Enniskillen and Limerick, and Irish soldiers made up half of the Company's white soldiers.

Once in India, the Irish became known as the 'rishtis' and were regarded as inferior to the English soldiers. They distinguished themselves by their brutality against the Indian people, asserting a status at least higher than theirs, if lower than that of the English. Rudyard Kipling's Kim – Kimball O'Hara – was a rishti, a child born to Irish parents who had gone native in India.

Irish men in India were not noted for any hint in their attitude to the Indians that they would later empathise with Indian nationalists. There was no brotherhood of the oppressed between them. Far from having difficulty identifying with Britain's colonial endeavours, these were the men who fought in Northern India in 1857 to crush a rebellion begun by sepoys, Indian soldiers in the employ of the East India Company.

In Delhi today there is a cemetery named after one of the Irish officers who was most brutal in crushing the rebellion, John Nicholson. Nicholson conducted several mass executions, often strapping rebel soldiers across the mouths of cannons and blowing them apart, though this practice was soon stopped because it was regarded as a waste of gunpowder. Nicholson died in the defence of Delhi. In 2019 I visited the Nicholson Cemetery and it was being restored. Nicholson's grave was ill-tended, but there was a sign directing tourists to it. The cemetery is still in use and the section where Christian burials continue is much tidier, the grass cut round the graves, the headstones polished and clean.

We might wonder why India would still allow Nicholson to be honoured. It would be equivalent to honouring the Black and Tans in Dublin. Are we Irish more touchy about the Empire than the Indians are? And if so, why?

Another indication of Irish cruelty towards Indians is cited by Bartlett in his chapter on 'Ireland and India'. He quotes the memoirs of a Connaught Ranger, Private Frank Richards, who describes the men as blatantly racist and casually brutal in their dealings with Indian people and says that, because of the way they used their boots and fists, they were more feared than any other British unit in India.

That same unit later provided republican tradition in Ireland with a martyr. James Daly was executed for mutiny in 1920, at a time when the IRA was harassing British forces in Ireland with a guerrilla campaign and British forces were carrying out reprisal atrocities. Daly's revolt within the Connaught Rangers is remembered today as a protest against the brutality of the Black and Tans. The Rangers were refusing to carry out soldiering duties until the British Army had left Ireland, so their weapons were taken into storage. Bartlett says that Daly and other Rangers had sought to seize weapons from a store and that two men were shot dead in a skirmish to recover them. He notes that, but for these deaths, the whole incident might have been dealt with more leniently. Instead, sixty-one Rangers were convicted of mutiny and fourteen were sentenced to death. In the end only one, Daly, was executed.

Bartlett questions Daly's motives for his actions. Yes, men were upset about the stories they were getting in letters from home about the behaviour of British forces, and the Black and Tans in particular, but Daly had signed up just a year earlier, when the War of Independence had already started. And Daly's execution, argues Bartlett, was not part of a British effort to punish Irish rebels, but had more to do with conditions in India, where they feared signalling to Indian soldiers that a mutineer might escape execution.

Daly's fellow mutineers were released from British prisons in 1923 after protests for political status, but the Irish government was slow to award them IRA pension rights. Cumann na nGaedheal's Ernest Blythe said sarcastically that 'their … patriotism was an afterthought'. When Daly's body, along with two others, was reinterred in Ireland in 1970, Daly's at Tyrellspass and the others at Glasnevin, the government was content to leave the funeral arrangements to the National Graves Association which tends IRA graves. Ruairí Ó Brádaigh, the president of Provisional Sinn Féin, led the ceremony. Daly's coffin was draped with the same tricolour that had covered the coffin of Terence MacSwiney, the Lord Mayor of Cork who died on hunger strike in 1920. The flag was brought for the occasion by Patrick O'Sullivan, whose brother Joseph was executed for assassinating Sir Henry Wilson in London in 1922.

Daly has been firmly established in the republican canon as a martyr. In 2021, at the unveiling of a memorial to the soldiers, President Higgins honoured the Connaught Ranger rebels for an 'extraordinary act of defiance', which has inspired drama and song. He said that we should not hold it against these men that they were members of the British Army: 'It is important to try and put ourselves into the circumstances of the people with all of their contradictions.'

He continued, 'How can we not seek to understand the attempts that people made in the conditions they had been reduced to in the absence of being an independent state? They exercised their choices making a fist of life. We don't abuse their experience and we don't abuse their words or their actions.' None of this meant, said President Higgins, that the Empire could be absolved of its cruelties because subject peoples had enlisted.

The leader of the Ulster Unionist Party (UUP) Doug Beattie responded to this by accusing President Higgins of 'peddling a myth'. Doug had been a captain in the British Army and served in Afghanistan among Irish-born British soldiers. He said:

> I am proud – as a modern-day soldier – to say that I stood beside and fought alongside Irishmen and women from both sides of the border. Indeed 10% of my regiment, fighting in Afghanistan in 2010, was from the Republic of Ireland. To say they joined for purely societal reasons is a myth that cannot be sustained through rational argument and by extension to say the Irish soldier from centuries ago did also falls short of fact.

He continued, 'It is simply wrong to judge the motivations and actions of people over a hundred years ago and more through the narrow prism of Irish nationalism in the modern era.'

Dan Harvey, like Doug Beattie, has sought to contend with the tailoring of history to suit an anti-British narrative. He commences his account of Waterloo with an interesting observation: 'If there is a place on earth that has defined its identity against the British, it is Ireland. So how was it that the Irish whom the British suppressed for centuries should have contributed so much to the Waterloo campaign and why has this participation largely escaped notice to date?' (Harvey, 2017, p. 1.)

While on my trip to Delhi in 2019, during which I visited the Nicholson Cemetery, I stayed at Maidens Hotel. This is a luxury colonial-era hotel favoured by British tourists. It boasts a Curzon Room in honour of a former British viceroy, which exhibits photographs of the Delhi Durbar to mark the accession of King George V.

I was in the Punjab a hundred years after the Amritsar massacre, when the Irish General Dyer, under an Irish lieutenant governor, O'Dwyer, murdered up to a thousand people engaged in a protest. There had been rioting for three days before the massacre. General Dyer had been able to confine the protest within a market area by sealing the exits before ordering his Gurkhas to open fire. The British acknowledged over 300 deaths, but local estimates put the number much higher. O'Dwyer gave official approval by telegram the following day.

Who were these ghastly men?

Sir Michael Francis O'Dwyer was a civil servant awarded the Most Exalted Order of the Star of India and the most Eminent Order of the Indian Empire. He was born in Tipperary in 1864 and educated by the Jesuits in County Offaly. He joined the Indian Civil Service at the age of eighteen, perhaps having few alternatives to being a burden on the large Catholic family in which he was raised. Education was his way out of poverty and he thrived on it.

General Reginald Dyer had no dark Irish childhood to overshadow his prospects or explain his cold, murderous temperament. He was born in India and sent to Ireland for his education in Cork and Dublin, before opting for Sandhurst and training as an army officer at the age of twenty-one. He got his first taste of riot control work in Belfast in 1886 during the protests that accompanied Gladstone's failed efforts to get Home Rule through parliament.

O'Dwyer was assassinated in London over twenty years after the massacre for his role in the slaughter. He was buried in Brookwood Cemetery with a Celtic Cross for a headstone.

We tell each other the story of Ireland's historic battles for freedom, but we exclude Irish participation in the Napoleonic wars, the American Civil War, the colonisation of India and many others. In fact, the story of the Irish at war is much more than just the record of occasional rebellions. And while we like to think of the Irish soldier as a noble and principled lover of freedom, when we look back we find him in the Boer Wars, at the Crimea and of course, in the trenches at Flanders. Judging by how Irish people expended their military energies, far more of it was to do with careerism, fighting for Britain or just reinforcing their sense of citizenship and responsibility in a new land. For instance, in the American civil war, Irish soldiers fought on both sides, for and against slavery.

To give some impression of Irish involvement, I searched for my father's and mother's surnames in the military databases. Dohertys and O'Hallorans fought in the Crimean War – 432 Dohertys and 48 O'Hallorans. In the Boer war, there were 35 O'Hallorans and 240 Dohertys. I also counted the Dohertys and O'Hallorans killed in the Irish War of Independence. Of the

Dohertys killed, four were in the IRA, three were in the Royal Irish Constabulary (RIC) and one was shot as an informer by the IRA.

My father's mother was a Kerr. Three Kerrs and one O'Halloran died in that war.

The dead Doherty who caught my eye first was Barney, because he had my father's name. Barney had been in the British Army during the First World War and his brother was killed at Gallipoli. In May 1920 there had been rioting for some days in Derry after the IRA killed a police inspector called Denis Moroney. After what appeared to be an end to the fighting, Barney offered to walk a girl home, which was decent of him. He was struck by a shot fired, presumably by a loyalist, and he collapsed and died in Linenhall Street. That same month twenty-four-year-old James Doherty, an RIC man, was 'accidentally shot by a comrade' in Donegal.

There was serious violence a few weeks later in Derry, with five people killed in two days. One of them was twenty-three-year-old James Doherty. He was at the wake house for one of the dead, chatting on the doorstep to Janie O'Kane. Janie saw a woman in Fountain Street point them out to a gunman. The gunman fired and killed James.

In October that year, Francis Doherty was killed as part of a six-man RIC patrol that was ambushed by the IRA. Another Doherty RIC man, John, was forty-seven years old and had been in the constabulary for twenty-five years. He was stationed in Westport, County Mayo and was part of a convoy of vehicles travelling through the most beautiful part of the country to Leenane in June 1921. I have cycled that road not knowing what horror took place there. The convoy was attacked by the

West Mayo Brigade of the IRA, and the RIC men and soldiers fought them off for over three hours. The IRA killed five policemen and, even after a three-hour battle, had time to pick up the police and army weapons, taking twenty-three rifles, twenty-five revolvers, one Lewis gun and 5,000 rounds of .303 ammunition.

This was before the invention of the helicopter.

A James Doherty lost an arm when serving with the Leinster Regiment. Then, on 25 June 1921, he was taken from his home in Limerick by armed men. When his body was recovered, the IRA said that he had been 'tried, convicted and duly executed' as an informer. His father said he had come under suspicion because he had been 'chummy' with the police.

Daniel O'Doherty worked in the family bicycle repair business. He was one of three men taken from their homes on the same night in April 1921 and shot dead in Dromore, County Tyrone. The forces of the state had no compunction then about picking up IRA suspects and killing them, often in reprisal for previous attacks on the army or police.

Edward Doherty from Ballybofey ran off when soldiers raided his house following an IRA ambush. They shot him dead.

The one O'Halloran who died was also a member of the IRA. Another IRA man called Thomas Blake had been shot dead three days earlier while walking home alone. There was fighting between mourners and the police at the funeral and shots were fired. One of those shots killed Patrick O'Halloran.

I haven't been trawling for Dohertys and O'Hallorans in various wars in order to find members of my own family. I have no way of connecting myself to these people. But by using these names that I know to look into past allegiances, what these findings tell me is that Irish people have not been uniformly anti-imperialist. I presume that if I took a few other random Irish names I would get similar results.

Daniel O'Connell and Patrick Pearse both claimed to speak for the Irish people, but if we define a people according to what they are ready to fight for, it is impossible to conceive of a coherent Irish sense of purpose. Nor could anyone ever speak for a whole nation. At the time when half the white soldiers in India were Irish, many more in the same army were Indian, so subject peoples joining the imperial army was fairly routine. O'Connell wanted to speak for Ireland when some of us were defending slavery and some opposing it. Pearse presumed to speak for all of us, when more were about to die in Flanders than in Dublin.

People identify themselves by the wars they commemorate. That's what determines whether you wear an Easter lily or a poppy in November. But you can only identify yourself according to your country's wars by ignoring some of them, and in the case of the Irish by ignoring the biggest ones. And how does this impact on the question of whether Ireland can be united as one country?

On the one hand, the diversity of Irish traditions, the legacy of our role in empire alongside our proud anti-imperialism suggests that we as a people might not knit well together. We have already seen signs of that in the first century of the state.

Some of those O'Dohertys in the British Army were uncles of mine. One deserted in 1943. He came home to Derry on leave and his mother burnt his uniform in the back garden and sent him into Donegal. Another was a prisoner of war in Italy. But these things were spoken of quietly and not shared with the neighbours, for the standard narrative of Irish nationhood was that our heroes were republicans and that those who fought for Britain had no significant part in the story.

That has been put right in recent years, up to a point. While there are memorials in Dublin now to the Irish dead of the First and Second World Wars, commemorating the Irish dead of the Great War has been particularly contentious because it overlapped with the Easter Rising.

And it's complicated. Many Irishmen joined up at the start of the First World War because they were encouraged to do so by John Redmond's nationalists. Some argue that these Irishmen had joined up to advance the claim for Home Rule and were therefore part of the broader sacrifice made for freedom. But even with that encouragement, proportionately fewer enlisted in Ireland than in other parts of the UK. Compared to 26 per cent of Scottish men of serving age who joined the British Army during that war and 24 per cent of Welsh men, only 10 per cent of Irish men did. The period of greatest enthusiasm was between August and December 1914 when 43,000 Irish men volunteered, half of them from Ulster. A year later, less than a quarter of that number were joining up (Winter, 1977).

However, despite these lower numbers, if the Dohertys and O'Hallorans and O'Connors and others knew their family histories and took out old family photograph albums and uniforms from their attics, they might find to their surprise that they had much in common and much to talk about with even the most chauvinistic of northern Protestants and Orangemen.

In *Imagined Communities*, Benedict Anderson speculates that a nation is formed out of fellow feeling, 'a deep, horizontal comradeship'. And out of that comradeship grows the willingness to die for your country. The sense of nationhood is built on a history of the sacrifices made at war, but here's an anomaly. More Irish people died in other people's wars than in their own, and most particularly for Britain.

5

CULTURE

IT WAS 4 July, at about half past five, and I was driving home listening to light classical music on Lyric FM, when the presenter played a request from 'Joe' to mark American Independence day. The song he chose had more to do with Irish independence: 'Kevin Barry', sung by Paul Robeson. There wasn't even a warning for people of a sensitive disposition to pull into a lay-by lest the shock overwhelm them. Up came the sombre deep tones of Robeson to honour the martyrdom of an eighteen-year-old Irish rebel who was hanged by the British for his part in ambushing an army supply lorry that had been sent to a bakery to pick up bread.

I had known this song off by heart when I was a child and had even stood at the front of the class and sung it. But though I knew the lines – 'all around that little bakery, sure they fought them hand in hand' – I didn't know much of the story. O'Halpin and Ó Corráin (2020, p. 209) called the operation 'a botched arms raid on a military ration party outside Monk's Bakery'. When the shooting started, Barry's comrades scarpered and soldiers caught him hiding under a military lorry trying to unjam his automatic. They had the decency not to shoot him.

At his trial Barry refused to recognise the court martial and he is acknowledged to have walked calmly to the gallows and died bravely. The ballad records that he wanted to die by firing squad, like a soldier, rather than be hanged like a dog. O'Halpin and Ó Corráin say that he wrote in a letter from prison that his Black and Tan guards had all 'been most kind', though the song says they tortured him.

I was surprised to hear this on a national radio station on an entertainment show. Aside from small community stations which are actually set up to honour republican culture, I think it is inconceivable that a rebel song like that would be played in Northern Ireland, and certainly not on the BBC. Not that a lot of people in the audience wouldn't hold Kevin Barry in high regard and have been deeply moved by the song, but a lot of others, probably many more, would be appalled by the endorsement of an IRA legend. And maybe as many again would simply regard it as insensitive to play something that would annoy others if not themselves.

So I asked RTÉ if they had received any complaints and they told me they hadn't. Not one. The press officer's statement said, 'Producers use their own judgement on what music to play in a given programme. Context is important of course.'

This was a very small incident, of no apparent significance to the producer or the audience, yet it suggests to me something about how the South is different from the North. For instance, Máiría Cahill has spoken of how she was rebuked for playing The Wolfe Tones on a radio station set up to support Féile an Phobail, the West Belfast Festival which is largely run by republicans. I can't work out the reasoning behind that when The Wolfe Tones usually round off the festival with a big concert.

Bobbie Hanvey used to play rebel songs on a programme on Downtown Radio in Belfast. These were songs picked by guests. Once he had the former IRA leader Ruairí Ó Brádaigh on his show. Ó Brádaigh requested a song called 'The Old Alarm Clock' by the Dubliners. This made a joke of bomb-making: 'I'll show you how my small machine can make the peelers dance.' Hanvey refused to play the song, but asked Ó Brádaigh what the most powerful weapon in his arsenal was.

'History,' said Ó Brádaigh. He might have added that the relaying of history through IRA propaganda songs was what weaponised it.

I asked Bobbie Hanvey how Downtown responded to him playing requests from paramilitary-linked guests. He said, 'There were complaints all right. You had to balance it. I played lots of Orange songs too.'

There are lots of little differences between North and South that you can pick up on by listening to broadcasters. For example, you can say 'fuck' on RTÉ more lightly than you can say it on the BBC, though it is often softened to 'feck'. But the biggest apparent cultural difference between the two is that in the North we have more sectarianism. And one of the biggest challenges for a new all-Ireland government would be taking over the management of that sectarianism from the Northern Ireland Executive and from the police.

If the South didn't have its own experience of sectarianism, it would be starting out afresh on the challenge of helping the two northern communities to adapt to each other. However, it does have some limited experience of religious bigotry to draw on. For a start, it was, for most of the last century, a Catholic state, virtually a theocracy. There was substantial discrimination against Protestants in public service and in the framing of legislation, even a recognised 'special place' for Catholicism in the Constitution. And Catholicism held exclusive truth, which contained an inherent contradiction: that God wanted you to love your neighbour, but that the same God was going to send your neighbours to hell to burn for all eternity if they did not become Catholics too. Evangelical Protestantism, of course, had a similar conviction that it alone harboured the truth, and through the Orange Order, had an influence over government appointments in the North (see Shea, 1981).

This type of thinking is still strong within northern evangelical Protestantism. They believe that they are saved and that all others who have not received the Lord Jesus as a personal saviour are going to burn. And they can look you in the face and tell you this with the sweetest good nature as they offer you another biscuit. But a shared cast of mind is not the same thing as a shared world view, though there have been some allegiances between conservative Catholics and the born again, such as in the opposition to liberal legislation like permitting abortion or same-sex marriage, the kind of laws which modern Ireland feels quite pleased about.

Protestantism in the North encompasses a surprising range of attitudes and practices. One of the clearest illustrations of this is the annual Orange Order parade through Belfast. This is a huge carnival, though Pride has perhaps been a little bigger in recent years. Both are hugely entertaining experiences for those who don't take offence.

Where I grew up in Riverdale, I used to wait for the parade to come over the railway bridge at Finaghy. First came the pulsing martial rhythms and the thundering drums. Then, because they were ascending the bridge from the other side, I saw the tops of the banners and, as the men reached the brow of the bridge, these would be caught by the breeze and lifted over their heads to billow almost level behind them as they descended towards me. After them flowed the river of hats and white shirts and Orange collarettes, part shielded by the banners until they were closer.

What a study of humanity they presented as they passed. There were the athletically dextrous boys tossing and twirling batons. There were the drummers beating the goatskins as if they hated them. Where did they get the strength? Then little drum bands and accordion bands, with girls in tartan skirts and caps, then the men of the lodges marching in solemn formation. You could see that some of them were exhausted and hungover from partying round bonfires the night before, while others were proud decent Protestant men who never touched a drop and were marching in honour of their God and their Queen. The louche one might carry the bowler hat in his hand because he was sweating, his white shirt open several buttons down. The proud, perhaps slightly tubby, older men marched with dignity and defied or concealed their natural exhaustion, for this was the one day of the year when they could be elevated among their people as loyal Ulstermen.

I was fascinated by these parades and perplexed by the audience that turned out for them. They were bacchanalian in contrast to our own little Corpus Christi parades, but they were, at heart, reverential; reverential of God, monarchy and history, and of a sense of distinctive heritage. And this reverence was expressed by the drunken lout looking on, fat old ladies waving Union Jacks, slack-bodied ancients wheeled out of nursing homes to have their spirits lifted, and surly hard men who watched on and considered that they might have to fight again.

There were professional lodges and officer-class lodges. Once, at a parade in Royal Avenue in Belfast before the Troubles, I saw an Orangeman of some military bearing and confidence leave the parade to berate two uniformed soldiers and order them to stand to attention while the parade passed, which they did, poor things.

The parades, then, were like a cross section of the whole of Protestant society, but of course there were a lot of people we call Protestant who were not there, who were perhaps still in bed, or wishing they could go downtown, if the shops were only open, to buy the latest Beatles or Led Zeppelin LP. When we talk in demographic terms we count them as Protestants too, or – as in the equality monitoring forms – 'perceived Protestants'.

There are positive and negative understandings of the Orange culture. Some say it is coat-trailing triumphalism, letting the taigs know who's on top. This view may indeed be shared by some of the Orangemen themselves. I once saw an Orange band practise outside a Catholic church during Mass, then turn smartly away as soon as the Mass was over. It had only one purpose and that was to disrupt the service within.

Others say Orangeism is a wholesome and dignified celebration of the religious freedoms won for Protestants and defended by the British monarchy. What is striking always about the parades is how they mix the generations and the classes, stolid upright Christian gentlefolk and a surly rabble.

Every year the Orange culture presents problems for the authorities and for neighbouring communities. Much of the population of Belfast takes its holiday at this time to be away from it all and to protect their children from it. You can meet young people who grew up in Belfast and have never seen the big parade.

Throughout the 1990s, deadlock over protests against parades going through areas in which they were not welcome became the sole preoccupation of the entire population for weeks at a time, generating murder, burnings, rioting and enormous police overtime. In more recent years the contention has been over bonfires on the night before the Twelfth. These have become enormous towers and the authorities have been so loath to intervene that we have seen the absurdity of the fire service turning up to turn their hoses on the houses close by, to protect them rather than risk the wrath of a mob by attempting to extinguish the fire itself.

In 2021 two executive ministers sought a court order to compel the police to dismantle a bonfire in Adam Street, Belfast, across the road from the Catholic New Lodge. The police argued that they could not intervene without risk of being petrol bombed and fired on. So apparently loyalists feel no shame in their arguments being won through the threat of violence. Meanwhile, bonfire organisers were setting out bouncy castles for the children – Protestant children – to enjoy themselves.

In the new Ireland after unification, all this would be Dublin's headache.

As Belfast waited to hear if the police would be forced against their own better judgement to move against the bonfire on Adam Street, I drove to Rossnowlagh in Donegal to see how the Orange culture fared there. This was during lockdown, so parades in the Republic were banned, but the Order had got around this by holding an open-air band practice and putting out word that people could come and watch it.

The venue I was directed to was a large sloping field on a hill opposite St John's Church of Ireland above Rossnowlagh. A steward was on hand to direct cars towards one side of the field for viewing and the bands to another side. There wasn't much to see when I arrived, just other cars backing up alongside mine, a big silvery sky busy with clouds and the trees that denied us a view of the hills to the north.

I was on my own, but most of the people arriving were old couples, and the treat in this day out was clearly as much in meeting each other again as in seeing the bands. My first attempt to introduce myself didn't go well. A man stood chatting to the driver of a car beside me and I went up to say hello. I said, perhaps tactlessly, 'I am a gatecrasher really. Are you expecting a good show? I'm new to this sort of thing.'

The man standing by the car was a thran lump. I think that's how you would say it in Ulster Scots. He was heftily built, especially in front, in an open-necked check shirt and trousers with a strong belt. I'd say he was in his sixties, which would make him younger than me, but he immediately impressed me as someone who assumed the authority of the years regardless of the age of the people he was dealing with.

He said absolutely nothing to me, so I shuffled around with some pretence of purpose and then sidled gently back to my car, picking up a thread of the conversation he resumed with the man in the other car. 'If you want to meet a couple of oul folk, go to church on Sunday. That's where you'll get them.'

This was clearly the challenge of their lives, meeting other old people to talk to, but not me. Well, I'm told I look young for my age.

The conversation on the other side of me was about the weather. This is what oul folk talk about with each other when meeting up after months parted by lockdown regulations.

'So long as it keeps dry.'

'We'd a right wee skift of rain earlier.'

At the other end of the field I could make out the members of a pipe band in kilts and white shirts, with wee military caps, getting out of their cars and mingling. Beyond I had a glimpse of the Blue Stack mountains. The breeze carried up towards us the refrain of 'Abide with Me'.

The field itself was well trimmed and the signs directing traffic and urging people to stay in their cars also marked out, more or less, a parade route, but for now the band was going nowhere and no one seemed to mind. Northerners and southerners were meeting and comparing lockdown regulations on different sides of the border.

'Begod if they told me I couldn't go more than five kilometres I'd get no shopping done at all for there is nothing nearer than ten kilometres to me.'

An ice cream van arrived. The band played 'Nearer My God to Thee'.

Nearer the ice cream van, I met the county grand master of Donegal, Davy Mahon. He was not in his regalia, just an open-necked yellow shirt. He explained that normally on the

Saturday before the Twelfth the Donegal Orangemen would rally in this field and then march down to the beach. I had seen them there in previous years enjoying an ice cream cone or paddling at the water's edge.

I had chatted one year with a stallholder who was selling little T-shirts that read, 'Keep Ulster Tidy, Dump Your Litter in the Irish Republic'. It would have been pedantic to point out to him that he was still in the province of Ulster, but that if he kept on going he'd have the pick of Leitrim and Sligo. We both knew what he meant.

Davy had no sense of apprehension about me being there. It might be possible to live most of your life in a neighbourhood in Belfast in which you would rarely meet a person from a different community. Indeed, most Catholics going about their business in parts of Donegal might never meet a Protestant, but a Protestant in Donegal would be meeting Catholics at every turn, in the shop, along the road, the postman at the door. So why wouldn't they be the most non-sectarian people you'd ever meet, having more acquaintance with both sides of the divide than the rest of us?

He told me that Donegal has seventeen Orange lodges and about 600 members. He struck me as having a tendency not to be specific. How long had he been the grand master? 'Aw, could be twenty years nearly.'

He continued, 'I have three or four children here in the local band and my sons and all belong to the lodge here. It's your [meaning 'our'] culture. You [meaning 'we'] are brought up in the Protestant faith and the Orange Order is part of it.'

Was there any friction in Donegal between the Orangemen and the wider community?

'Naw, we would never see friction here, like.'

Davy is a rich businessman. 'I would do a lot of business with Roman Catholics. Property business and I have holiday parks. I have lots of businesses like. I've a lot of good friends Roman Catholics. It makes no difference to me like. Business is business.'

He lives now in Kesh in Northern Ireland and votes for one of the unionist parties there, but he grew up in Donegal and went to school at Kilbarron in Ballyshannon, a school run by the Church of Ireland. He learned the Irish language at school but says, 'Whatever I had to learn, aye. I never was very fond of it like. But I learned it anyway. It never did me any harm.'

He supports the British monarchy and sees no contradiction between that and his Irish citizenship. He says Protestants in Donegal tended in the past to vote for Fine Gael, but that now many of them vote for Fianna Fáil. 'They would vote for whatever party does things for them probably. There's plenty of members voting Fianna Fáil, maybe fifty-fifty, I'm not sure.'

But he says that Orange lodges are disadvantaged through not having strong political connections:

> A lot of our Orange halls would have got very little grant aid or any funding that way. We get no funding for our demonstration in Rossnowlagh every year. We apply to the local council but we never get any. Or from the government. It costs a lot of money for just till run that day like but never no funding.

As we were speaking, the Moyne pipe band ascended the hill behind us, the band leader a young woman twirling her baton and looking boldly ahead. This was lovely. A gorgeous sunny day in a field in Donegal with friendly people and a bit of a carnival atmosphere. What could anyone see wrong with it?

In Belfast there would have been someone handing out tracts urging us to be saved, or there would have been a unionist politician working through the crowd shaking hands and canvassing votes. There would be few votes for a northern party here. Or there might have been speeches as much of castigation as celebration.

I had left Belfast with the expectation that the bonfires would be lit that night or the next, depending on whether the loyalists who'd built them would be honouring the sabbath. Davy says, 'Just city areas, you know. Different way of working like. I don't know if it will ever change.' That's his analysis.

Does he think there will ever be a united Ireland? 'Nobody can say never to anything, but I can't see it in the near future anyway. While I'm living in Northern Ireland I'll be voting to stay in the Union.'

Maybe it was because the band was alongside us now that he kept his answers brief and didn't take the bait to enter a deeper political discussion. Or maybe that is the way a minority Orange culture conducts itself in the interests of not annoying anyone. That's what we were told as Catholics in Belfast in the past – don't be stirring things. Keep your thoughts to yourself.

For instance, I approached another man that day and asked him if he was an Orangeman, and his answer surprised me. He was defensive on first contact as if worried that our conversation might lead to argument. He said, 'Well. I'll not pretend I'm not.'

Did Davy think Ireland would ever go back into the Commonwealth?

He said, 'I think it would be nice, but I don't know if it's important or not. It's not an issue for me like.'

Is anything an issue for him, I wondered; anything at all?

'I don't really have any issues, so long as there is peace in the country, that's all we want.'

6

PROTESTANTS

ONE INDICATION OF how well the Irish Republic would absorb the Protestants of Northern Ireland is the country's past experience of assimilating Protestants, such as the Orange Order members in Donegal. There have been several recent studies arguing that the Republic failed to fully regard Protestants as citizens of the Republic and that neglect and humiliation of Irish Protestants has led to a depletion of their culture.

An horrific story in recent times is that of Eden Heaslip from Crosskeys in County Cavan. Eden was bullied at school by boys who taunted him for being a Protestant who should go back to 'his own country'. Eden took his own life. The Samaritans and others advise that we should not attribute his suicide to one cause, but his father, a Protestant married to a Catholic, clearly thought sectarianism played a part in it.

There are numerous stories of Protestant disaffection in the South in Deirdre Nuttall's book, *Different and the Same* (2020). It records stories of schoolchildren who were scoffed at by their peers as 'proddy woddy'. One tells of how, when they were going to school on holy days when the Catholics were off, the bus conductor would charge full fare, insisting that the schools were closed and that the usual discount for pupils did not apply.

I spoke to a friend of Protestant extraction and asked her if she would discuss her experience with me, but she says that as she has not been religious since her childhood, she is just the wrong person to ask. She may be counted among those who were lost to Irish Protestantism, although she has no sense herself of having lost anything. She has not been absorbed into a Catholic community or milieu but, if into anything, a secular world in which religious roots count for little and which is now large enough to allow her to feel free and normal.

Victor Griffin, who was Dean of St Patrick's cathedral in Dublin for over twenty years, often said that Protestants in the republic 'kept their heads down', being too small a minority to be seriously troublesome. The state did not need to oppress them because they simply didn't have the numbers to raise ardent protest, unlike the Catholic minority in the North, who could express their disquiet and umbrage on a scale that would require the state to take notice, to repress or adapt.

He wasn't the first to make that observation. Bolton Waller, a Protestant campaigner for Home Rule and later for Irish unity, argued in his pamphlet *Hibernia* (1928) that Irish Protestants had been docile and had reneged on the prospect of contributing to the new Irish state (quoted in Morrissey, 2020). He accused them of 'timidity combined with superciliousness' and said, 'Having been so long denounced as a tyrannical "Ascendancy" they seem now – to avoid odium – to have gone to the opposite extreme … content to display a vague amiability rather than to make any definite contribution.'

On occasions Protestants did try to influence change but

with little effect. Historian Conor Morrissey recounts how a Church of Ireland delegation was received by the Minister for Justice, James FitzGerald-Kenney, when it tried to talk him into moderating new censorship laws in 1929. Morrissey draws on Peter Martin's study, *Censorship in the Two Irelands, 1922–39* (2006). The minister told the delegation that he wanted to ban anything attacking the institution of marriage or promoting contraception. Bolton Waller, who was on the delegation, told him that a large number of Protestants 'do absolutely genuinely and sincerely regard this as an intolerant and unfair bill'. Protestants were learning that there was little point in them pleading for special consideration in a Catholic state.

The Rev. Ian Paisley, the firebrand sectarian preacher who, with Desmond Boal, founded the DUP, often claimed that the new Irish state had committed genocide against Protestants. In his view, one strong reason for refusing a united Ireland was this evidence that Protestants would be persecuted and driven out as they had been before. Clearly this is absurd, but more reasoned arguments have been made that the new Irish state and its relationship with the Catholic Church did contribute to the depletion of Protestant congregations and communities.

There have been several books recently on Protestant experience, including Robin Bury's *Buried Lives: The Protestants of Southern Ireland* (2017). These publications defy the Irish essayist Hubert Butler's claim in his 1954 work 'Portrait of a Minority' that 'We Protestants of the Irish Republic are no longer very interesting to anyone but ourselves.' (Republished in Butler, 1986.) Bury says that while Protestants, as 3 per cent of the population in 2011, were by then an insignificant minority, they had played a significant role in Irish life, not least in providing some of the greatest Irish writers, from Swift to Beckett.

A sense had been generated through constitution and culture that the real Irish were Catholic and that the Protestants were like the rump of an enemy garrison. Not only had their numbers been depleted, but they had been stripped of land through legislation which compelled the old landlords to sell up to their tenant farmers. This is not usually represented as an injustice in accounts of the Irish nineteenth century, with most authorities agreeing that a parasitic class had been responsible for horrific poverty and hunger.

Butler argues that other European countries have managed to preserve the heritage and architecture of displaced and obsolete regimes while in Ireland much of this heritage was destroyed. For instance, in Austria the palaces of the Habsburgs were maintained and are now valued tourist attractions. In contrast, in Ireland, according to Bury, 300 of the big houses were burned down during the War of Independence, while up to 40,000 Protestants left the country.

Butler's portrait of the Protestant minority in the Republic depicts them as people who have given up the struggle to be noticed and taken account of. He represents them through a 'Mrs A', who is really quite content and has no wish to make a fuss about censorship or the divorce laws. Problems like that can be resolved with a trip to England. At the time he was writing, abortion was illegal there too, so that question didn't feature. Mrs A would probably have fainted at the suggestion.

There was the *Ne Temere* decree eating away at Protestant congregations with the demands of bishops granting dispensations that children of interfaith marriages be raised as Catholics. Not making a fuss about this, said Butler, was often about keeping the peace within the extended family. A Protestant family that rose up in rage against a bishop demanding that children of a mixed marriage should be raised as Catholic might have had a legitimate quarrel with the Church and the state which gave it a special position, but it would also find awkward silences on family occasions like Christmas dinner. The choice might be between social revolution and family harmony.

Butler said, 'A whole community can die without drama.' He argued that his people's 'amiable inertia' and 'refusal to express grievances or cherish hopes about Ireland' were actually delaying the only outcome that would reconcile two communities in Ireland. In his view that was Irish unity. He believed that in an all-Ireland parliament Protestants would have significant power and influence, but that the Protestant in the Republic had lost all hope of that, aware that the Protestants in Northern Ireland plainly didn't want it.

In 1954 Butler could still anticipate, or at least imagine, an Anglo-Irish voice being raised again. In his essay he represents the northern Protestant through the image of Colonel Topping, the Unionist Party's Chief Whip at Stormont. Topping had travelled to Kilkenny, where Butler was born, to participate in debates, to the horror of the *Kilkenny People*, which regarded his invitation as 'an insult to our patriot dead'.

Northern unionism in those days was led by an aristocratic class with which the Anglo-Irish Protestants in the South sought some affinity. Today the communities are still further removed from each other. The unionists of today are not from the aristocracy. Unionism itself has rebelled against the Big House and the plummy-voiced leaders it had up to the 1970s; people like James Chichester-Clark and Captain Terence O'Neill. Unionism is now led by a generation which, like the nationalists and republicans, has thrived on free education and has given up drawing on a landed aristocracy for authority. The last relic of that reverence for inherited right is their regard for the British monarchy.

Paul Burgess is a novelist and academic. He is a senior lecturer in applied social studies at University College Cork. He grew up a Protestant on the Shankill Road in Belfast and played with punk band Ruefrex. Paul says he believes that northern Protestants in particular, and northerners in general, 'will always be viewed by southerners with a degree of trepidation. Certainly by people of my vintage [Burgess is in his sixties]. I think even southern Protestants, born and raised in the Republic, are also still somewhat perceived as "kicking with the other foot". Not in an overt way but it's there.'

Sometimes it is overt but not confidently complained about.

I spoke to a northern Protestant man, who wouldn't let me name him or the person at the heart of his story. He told me he worked for a large organisation in Dublin where a senior member of staff harassed him almost daily:

> Virtually every time I had dealings with this guy, he would make snide remarks about my religion. For some reason I kept thinking, 'This must be what it's like being picked on by a prefect at an English public school'. It had that feel to it. It was really nasty venomous stuff but done in a sneering half-joking kind of way. As if he

was very conscious of maintaining plausible deniability if he ever needed it.

This man was regularly called an 'orange bastard' at work. But the same man says this abuse was an exception to the way he was treated by others and that his own colleagues were appalled when they found out about it:

> But there was a long-established culture of fear in the company, so they said nothing. They would just drop their heads until he walked away. To be fair, I don't blame them. A complaint would have gone nowhere. It would have been scorned, 'Oh he's only joking with you', and a few weeks later I'd have lost my job on some pretext.

If we are asking whether a united Ireland is in prospect, we have to consider how well the communities of North and South might integrate with each other. Paradoxically, Paul Burgess – who, incidentally, is not the man at the heart of that story – thinks that his northern Protestant friends have been received better in Cork than northern nationalists. 'Interestingly, for many of my Belfast friends, it seems that perceptions of northern nationalists (as threatening, aggressive agitators) vary wildly from southern nationalists (welcoming, civilised, good craic, more quintessentially "Irish" in the positive stereotypical sense).'

In the mid-1980s the northern writer Sam McAughtry took off from Tiger's Bay, the loyalist part of Belfast he grew up in, to explore 'the Free State' and found Cork similarly uncongenial towards northern nationalists then. He visited a Belfast family which had fled Belfast to get as far away as possible from the Troubles and the danger of their children becoming indoctrinated by IRA thinking. Nuala Laverty told McAughtry, 'Maybe you might see a tiny bit of support for the Provos over on the north side amongst the poor people, but this place couldn't care less about the north. For dear's sake, that's what attracted us to it in the first place. What we didn't know was that they would be capable of such coldness to outsiders.' (McAughtry, 1987, p. 155.)

Another northern woman living in Cork told Sam, 'Even knowing that I have lived here for twelve years, the people at work still regard me as an IRA sympathiser. It's kept low, this attitude, but it rears its head every time there is any kind of outrage committed in the North.'

Paul Burgess says that if northern nationalists think they are to be 'the midwife to any future unity', they might find their efforts under-appreciated: 'Their expectations of welcome and acceptance in ROI are much more likely to be disappointed, and more hurtfully so. A bit like how Ulster Protestants feel that they are the unwanted children of the Union. That being said, I think all northerners are somewhat viewed as "wayward" children but part of the extended family nonetheless.'

When his northern and southern friends socialise, he thinks both sides take care not to raise sensitive issues that might lead to argument: 'Irish people, north and south, are incredibly skilled in finding common cause and avoiding the discussion of intractable politics/identity, should it offend. But my experiences are almost exclusively drawn from sociable contexts. And reasonable people!'

Paul regards himself as a reasonable person. He wrote songs against sectarianism when playing with Ruefrex. Before doing his PhD in Cork and taking a post at the university in 1993, he was a local government community relations officer in the North and a researcher in Belfast for the 1992 Opsahl Commission, which sought ideas for resolution in Northern Ireland that might attract broad support.

Yet his sense that the South would never quite embrace a northern Protestant, anti-sectarian liberal writer was made concrete by a visit from the police.

'Two burly detectives arrived, shirtsleeve order on a hot day, clipboards in hand. "The thing is ..." explained the more brusque of the two, "... we`ve had an anonymous tip-off to our Crimeline service. The Anti-Terrorist Squad have been given your name as someone involved in the [UVF] terrorist murder at The Widow Scanlan's Pub in Dublin."'

He was appalled.

I'm guessing that the Guards didn't really think he was likely to be a loyalist paramilitary sleeper. If so, they would not have risked signalling to him that his cover had been blown without first running a check on him with the Police Service of Northern Ireland (PSNI). But that doesn't account for their rudeness to him, whereas sectarian bigotry might.

Another Protestant who has spent a long time in the South is Davy Adams. Davy was a real loyalist, a member of the Ulster Defence Association, an armed group that murdered Catholics, and later of the political party that grew out of that movement, the Ulster Democratic Party. He participated in the negotiations towards the Good Friday Agreement. Afterwards, the party got little electoral support and he took to journalism as a commentator on BBC Radio Ulster's *Talkback* programme. For ten years he was a columnist for *The Irish Times*.

Davy has a light and affable nature, and he is a thoughtful guy. After one column he wrote for *The Irish Times*, he got a call from John O'Shea, the founder of the charity Goal, that led to an invitation to him to travel to developing countries where Goal was working. And that led to him being offered a job in the media department of Goal in Dún Laoghaire.

He says now:

> And to be perfectly honest, I wouldn't have held it against people if they had had problems working with me. If the role had been reversed, say a republican of my background had landed into a part of Belfast, even not necessarily one of the loyalist areas but generally, from the republic to work, I doubt whether he or she would have been made as comfortable and welcome as I was. That's just being upright honest about it.

The office staff could easily google him and learn about his background:

> There were those who thought it was a real novelty. They didn't say that, but you could tell. And they were great. Then you had a substantial number who were thinking, who cares? Let's see what he's like. Then there was a group who, very understandably, were not very standoffish, but enough that I could realise they were waiting to see what sort of person I was. They were cautious, wary of becoming too friendly.

He said, 'All of that soon disappeared. Once people get to know you as Davy, that's it.'

What struck me talking to Davy at home outside Belfast was that he would not have pleaded injustice if some of his colleagues had chosen to shun him because he had been a loyalist. He says he would have accepted that. The other thing is that, as we talked, he came very slowly round to revealing instances in which he *was* treated badly. He seemed actually to have forgotten about them.

One was an occasion when two republicans stalked him. They would eyeball him unnervingly as he walked to his office along the Dún Laoghaire seafront. After this began to look more like threat than curiosity, he spoke to the security staff at Goal, who brought in the gardaí. A detective identified those harassing him as members of Sinn Féin and got them to back off.

I think the genuine reason why these worrying instances of abuse and harassment feature so lightly in Davy's account of his experience is that he loved Dublin and made lasting friendships there, like Dave the painter. The two Dave's were smokers and would step outside for a cigarette and a yarn:

> One day he said to me that his mother had read a big piece I had written for the *Daily Mirror* from Syria, and she'd said to Dave, 'Do you know this guy?' 'Oh aye,' says Dave, 'A great friend of mine.' And Dave told me that his mother would go and light a candle for me every time I was heading off somewhere. I never met the woman, but she loved the piece that much.

Dave the painter would routinely ask, 'Any word of you going off Davy? The mudder was askin' after ye.' And if he said he was going away, she would be straight down to the church to light another candle and say a prayer that he'd be safe.

His impression of other Protestants in the Republic is that they are now fully assimilated, but that it wasn't always so: 'The Protestants I got to know were very integrated and very Irish but not without a passed-down memory of it not always being like that.'

He worked with some Protestants without knowing at first that they were Protestants because the secret signalling that comes so easily to northerners isn't part of how Dubliners interact with each other.

'You know what it is like being from here. Your antenna is so sharp.'

*

Neale Richmond, a Fine Gael TD from South Dublin, is a Protestant with relations in Northern Ireland. He is also committed to working for a united Ireland. He is aware of discrimination against Protestants in the Republic as part of their historic experience rather than as a present problem.

He met me in Belfast, in a cafe over a bookshop, on one of the wettest winter days. I was sitting opposite him shivering in my damp trousers, having walked into town, and he was groomed and fresh in the smart suit that a politician who has more important business than meeting a journalist is expected to wear. He had other appointments after me at the same table.

He recalled:

> My generation was not discriminated against, but you
> would have got the bit of sectarian abuse, casual graffiti
> on the walls of the school. You'd have played matches
> against certain schools. It was never nasty.
>
> When I went to university in UCD I was exposed to
> a bit of a broader audience and got to know people from
> more diverse backgrounds. I wouldn't call it a sheltered
> childhood, far from it, but when the kids on my road
> were going to hurling, I was going to hockey. But I lived
> in a part of Dublin where there was a large Protestant
> population proportionately.

As he describes it, there are marked cultural distinctions
between Protestants and Catholics rather than differences of
opinion on the constitution.

> I felt I had a different insight into the North. We spent
> a lot of time going up to the North as kids. We would
> spend most of our summers up at my granny's in Cavan
> and when you were there you would hop across to do an-
> ything because there was nothing to do. If you wanted a
> swim you would go to Enniskillen. Or if we were visiting
> relations, they were all living north of the border, some
> along the border, some in Downpatrick, Ballynahinch, in
> south Belfast itself.

But he wasn't as clued in as a northern-born kid on how things
worked there:

I remember in July 1990, Ireland were playing in the soccer world cup. I was still at primary school and I had a Jack-the-lad outfit that included tricolour shorts, which I wore religiously for about two months until the morning we were going up to visit our cousins in Ballynahinch and I couldn't find them anywhere. My mother had hidden them. When we arrived at the house I said, why are they all supporting France? Because there were red, white and blue kerbstones.

Often as a teenager he wore a poppy in commemoration of the British and Commonwealth war dead: 'Armistice Day at school had a large war memorial, as does the IRFU and lots of others. I was getting into the car and my mum said, "Be sure to take that off." Not as in I don't want you wearing it but as in you'd never know what someone might say to you.'

That 'whatever you say, say nothing' culture was strong.

'I remember Ken Maginnis being in our rugby club once because he was president of Dungannon.' Maginnis was an Ulster Unionist MP and a former soldier in the Ulster Defence Regiment.

And as a petulant teenager – I know him from the telly, sort of thing – this was before the Good Friday Agreement – I wanted to ask him about politics and my dad said, 'Look you don't talk about politics in a rugby club.' The man's here on rugby business, he's having a drink, we're watching a match – that's just sheer politeness.

So keeping your opinions guarded was not just a caution in the company of Catholics, but also of northern Protestants.

Incidentally, Ken Maginnis went on to be a strong defender of the Good Friday Agreement and a member of the House of Lords. He was disgraced and suspended from the house on accusations of bullying. He has a pretty brash manner and a stubborn nature, little inclined towards apology, but I have enjoyed his company many times and wonder now how Neale Richmond's political thinking might have evolved if he had indeed squared up to him and received a succinct summation of northern political realities in return.

The Richmonds were not staunchly Fine Gael, but they were that way inclined. There was political discussion in the home and often a hush for a few days after a serious bomb in Northern Ireland. His mother might say, 'That was a bit close to your cousin Graham.'

His mother was appalled by some Protestant behaviour there, particularly around the protest against the Holy Cross Primary School in north Belfast, when a blast bomb was thrown at police protecting small children trying to get to school.

Neale notes how Protestants have found their way into all the southern political parties:

> Protestants have popped up in every party, but you think of the really strong Protestant politicians in the south, Ivan Yates, Billy Fox, Heather Humphries. The Dockrells were the last unionist politicians in Dublin, in 1918. One of the Dockrells is now a councillor in my area. The son of one of them subsequently joined Cumann na Gael and Fine Gael. Trevor Sargent, a former leader of the Green

party – his father was a clergyman. Robert Dowds in the Labour party. He would have come through the teaching unions, and Church of Ireland.

But unionism as a political idea in the Republic has gone. 'No one harks back to the days of the Union, but they hark back to what was, I suppose, the societal tenets of unionism, the sports we played, the schools we went to, the churches we went to.'

He does not think that Irish Protestants have conflicted allegiances to Britain and Ireland: 'We wouldn't have had an issue with having a silver jubilee tea caddy. There would have been a lot of that in my grandparents' house. Allegiance or a sense of being a subject? Probably not. And if you ask them, they are all Irish first, but they wouldn't have been anti-British.'

And his connections with Northern Ireland have come in handy politically. When Leo Varadkar as Taoiseach met with Orange Order leaders, he asked Neale to join them:

> They all knew me before I got there, and not through being the politician. They knew of my granda, and they knew my uncle Jim – as we call him – and one of them had just visited him in the nursing home. One of them was working in Clondalkin in a meat processing plant. I said, do the lads in the meat processing plant know you're an Orangeman? And he said aye, but half of them are east Europeans.
>
> They were all from a farming community. One of them had been to school with a friend of mine.

He finds that Protestants north and south are interconnected with family links, associations through church, school and sports clubs, and that their identity is now founded on those associations rather than on a determination, like northern Protestants, to declare themselves British:

> I think the identity and the role of the Queen is really secondary to that connect with the community, and I think with the general Protestant community that has remained. The politics are all different; they go from Green, Fine Gael, Labour but, not to be sectarian about it, there is a huge Protestant population in my constituency. They are not going to vote for me purely because I'm a Protestant, but they're like, we know him, he went to school with my son, or his parents were lovely or he played rugby and sure he's one of ours, we'll give him a scratch. And I get that on the doors.
>
> Heather gets it as well. Ivan Yates got a bit of it, but even Trevor Sargent used to get a bit of it. Another cousin who was a primary school principal in Malahide says, of course I voted for Trevor, his dad was a clergyman. Why not? And he's such a nice guy.

He believes that his nationalism is pragmatic and unthreatening. His biggest concern, he says, is that a border poll could be thrust on us at any time by a chaotic British government playing for distraction. He, therefore, wants preparations now for that eventuality, the development of a conception of what a united Ireland might be like so that people know what they are voting for. The example of how these things can go wrong is the Brexit

referendum, in which the simple question didn't incorporate
any vision of the complexity of what might follow.

> I think we could be voting on this in the next decade.
> That's not necessarily my desire. I have been slated by re-
> publicans on social media because I got up at Féile and I
> said the general consensus in '98 was that we'd not be vot-
> ing on anything for at least a generation. That's ten years
> on from now. Realistically, if we are voting on this within
> thirty years of the Good Friday Agreement, so be it.

*

The polar opposite of Neale Richmond, a Protestant who wants
a united Ireland, might be Chris Hudson, who grew up as a
southern Catholic from a republican family but now argues
against unification. Today, Chris is a Unitarian clergyman of
the most liberal possible theology. He is minister of All Souls,
near Queen's University Belfast, a non-subscribing presbyterian
congregation.

Chris grew up in Dún Laoghaire. He has been a hairdresser,
a trade union organiser and later a clergyman, but in the 1960s
he was the teenage child of a family that revered the republican
tradition. He says:

> I thought I was part of a narrative for most of my early
> years. My father told me a story about how the Irish
> people were the aborigines of Ireland and that I should
> be proud of my family because they took part in the fight
> for independence to the extent that one of them died in

the Irish Civil War. So we were a noble people and we struggled against British imperialism, particularly the English and then we were sold out by the Free Staters and Michael Collins got his due reward as far as my father was concerned. It didn't come quick enough, in fact. And I passionately bought into that as a young man.

He even went with a friend to the Sinn Féin Headquarters in Gardiner Place in Dublin to try to join the IRA: 'They told me I was too young and they told my friend he wasn't suitable because he had a limp. So much for the equality agenda. We never did join.'

When he organised a rally in honour of Roger Casement in 1966, he recognised that many people around him had little interest in a fading legend of Ireland's heroic struggle for freedom: 'My sister was embarrassed because I had a tricolour flying from the house. She thought it would bring down the neighbourhood.'

At the same time that he was struggling to impress on his peers the need to keep retelling the story that shaped the nation, others felt excluded. If you were Protestant in Ireland there was little space for you in that story. The leaders of the 1916 Rising had declared themselves to be Catholic. Even James Connolly, the socialist, recovered his faith before his execution. One of Chris's concerns is to remind people in the Republic of ingrained sectarianism there.

He recalls, 'As a trade unionist I represented Protestants who were discriminated against, including one woman who couldn't even say in her workplace that she was a Protestant because they would jeer at her. And they wouldn't think they would jeer at her. She said, "They make remarks about Protestants. They think I am a Catholic.'"

Once when he was involved in mediation work between Irish officials and Ulster loyalists, he was seen in a pub with the Progressive Unionist Party leader David Ervine. Ervine was popular, despite his background as an Ulster Volunteer Force (UVF) bomber and prisoner, and was often approached in public by strangers who had seen him on the media and trusted him as sincere in his efforts to bring peace.

Chris says:

> A woman came up and said to him, 'I'm a big fan of yours'. They all loved David. Then she said, 'You know David, the one thing about down here is we don't care about religion.'
>
> And David said, 'Oh, is that right?'
>
> She said, 'You know, I was working with a young fellow and about three weeks ago his father died. We never knew he was a Protestant until the day of the funeral.'
>
> And I said, 'That's interesting, So he never could bring himself to tell you he was a Protestant?'

He tells me another story of an English woman who took a case against an employer for discrimination and the judge accepted that she had been discriminated against as a woman but not as a Protestant. He ruled that as a member of the Church of England, she would not have understood the abusive terms used about her, that she was a 'jaffa'.

'The point was that if she couldn't understand the abusive terms she couldn't have taken offence at them.' He adds that, in general, 'to be fair, there would not have been discrimination against Protestants to any great extent'.

Chris's political thinking had evolved away from republicanism towards socialism expressed in trade union activism. His religious thinking changed also and he gave up on Catholicism and, for a time, all religious belief. Then he was drawn to a Unitarian church and became a lay preacher while working as a full-time trade union official. He was ordained a minister in 2005 and posted to All Souls in Belfast. He is now moderator of the small but influential non-subscribing Presbyterian Church of Ireland.

He says now, 'I was motivated by my sense of dealing with and helping other people, a certain symmetry with my union work. There was no sense of divine revelation or bright lights, but there was epiphany in that I did begin to rediscover my own understanding of a relationship with God, in a universalist way.'

He is not remotely dogmatic in his religious beliefs and teaching:

> Yes community is at the heart of my religion and congregation but equally, without always spelling it out, faith matters. I love the fact that we have people in All Souls who accept the Jesus story as fact and those who see it in more poetic understanding teaching us to have a moral centre. We are an eclectic mix in every way, background and faith, that does appeal very strongly to me.

Once at a press conference I asked him if he believed in God and he said, 'Don't ask difficult questions.'

He has found a niche for himself as a liberal Christian in a city which has plenty of conservative evangelicals. He has walked in Pride parades and appeared eagerly in the media to say that his Church is happy to marry gay couples, this at a time when the Presbyterian Church in Ireland was shunning the Church of Scotland for baptising the children of gay couples. The Presbyterians sacked Steven Smyrl, an elder in Christ Church Sandymount, Dublin, because he was in a same-sex marriage. Steven said later, 'It was so hurtful. To be told that I was just dismissed and to have had every argument put to them over six months utterly ignored, it was really like a kick to the stomach.'

Chris Hudson has built up a congregation of liberal Christians who are probably more interested in community than in strict dogma. He says, 'I get people coming here to get their baby baptised or to get married and more often than not there is a Protestant and a Catholic sitting there, and clearly I would be very hard put to give you any idea of what their politics are.'

Chris isn't the type of clergyman to raise problems when people want support or prayer, although there are numerous stories told in Northern Ireland, and probably in the Republic too, of clergy who do raise theological objections or liturgical complications when, for instance, divorced people or a same sex couple want to marry, even still occasionally when a Protestant and a Catholic want to marry. I have seen him lead a baptism where he asked the congregation to welcome the child among them and to commit to being helpful in future when needed.

Despite his background, he has closer connections with Protestant communities than with Catholic. In part this follows from the work that he did during the early peace process to mediate between loyalists and the Irish government. But there is more to it than that: 'All my reference points, growing up in Dún Laoghaire, point not to west Belfast but to Holywood, County Down. I am more comfortable in Holywood.' Holywood is a middle-class satellite town of Belfast.

'Sometimes Catholics joke because I have a Dublin accent that I sound like a priest and that they are comfortable with that and even though it is a Protestant church it is not as Protestant as others.'

He says he represents people who feel that the churches they grew up in are no longer a good fit for them, spiritually, religiously or in a community. And he has observations about the difference between Catholics and Protestants which aren't far from the easy stereotype that Catholics write the poetry while Protestants build the tractors:

The Catholic faith is about mystery, the transubstantiation, the virgin birth. Prods don't really believe in that, and Presbyterianism, when you are involved with it, is not a lot about what you believe, it's more about the governance and who'll be the moderator and that sort of thing. There'll be big theological debates but it's not about the mysticism.

I did a sermon once on, *Is there an Ulster Protestant mystic*? Was C.S. Lewis the nearest thing to a Protestant mystic from Northern Ireland? The congregation laughed and said, you're wired to the moon, Chris. There is no such thing as a Protestant mystic. We cross every T and dot every I.

Meeting people like Chris Hudson, Neale Richmond, Davy Adams and Paul Burgess and others reminds me that the category 'Irish Protestant' covers individuals who are formed in their thinking more by experience than by background identity. So we can't always predict on the basis of their current religious or political beliefs how people will vote in a border poll that is still likely to be more than a decade away.

7

THE LANGUAGE

A COMMON COMPLAINT by Protestants interviewed in various books about how well they were assimilated or not as citizens of the Irish Republic is that they were forced to learn Irish. They did not identify with the project to re-gaelicise the country, and while many Catholics and others might have been similarly uncomfortable with a plan to make Irish a viable 'first official language', Protestants had the added alienating force of a distinctly ungaelic legacy. They felt the compulsion to learn it as a painful imposition and discrimination against them.

Regardless of the constitutional status of Irish, the real first language of Ireland is English. It is through English that most of our writers have distinguished themselves. Most Irish radio and television programmes are in English, as are most newspapers and magazines.

The Irish attachment to the old language and the remaking of it for the modern world is a legacy of a failed effort to create a Gaelic nation. It has nothing to do with facilitating communication, which is what languages are usually for. Fintan O'Toole, in a column in *The Irish Times* on 18 September 2021, claimed that the proclaimed love of Irish by most people in

Ireland is a form of virtue signalling comparable to their past determination to ban abortion through the constitution and their professed desire for a united Ireland. Confronted with the practical implications, he argued, the Irish quickly back away from these aspirations, as they backed away from the ban on abortion after a child was barred from leaving the country to end an unwanted pregnancy.

Irish is important to us but most of us won't do the work of actually learning it. As a badge of identity, most of us would not like to see it die out, but we'll not be the ones to make a concerted effort to save it. In the 2016 census, 1,761,420 people answered 'yes' to being able to speak Irish to some extent, but just under 7,700 forms were completed in Irish, less than half a per cent of the claimed gaeilgeoirí being able to manage that (www.rte.ie/documents/news/census-2016-summary-results-part-1-full.pdf, p. 66).

Other countries have succeeded in reviving an old language. The most impressive example is probably Israel. Chris Hudson says:

> Jews from all over the world, were allegedly coming home, speaking all different languages, so they cleverly revived Hebrew. There was a debate about that even in Israel, whether they should do it or make English the spoken language, or Arabic for that matter, but they revived a version of Hebrew and everybody learned that. It's an incredible success story.
>
> I think they did it because they were more committed to it.
>
> Somebody said to me on social media, my language

was stolen from me, and I said, have you reported it to the police? What does that mean? My father would say, the Irish will do anything for the language but speak it.

Still, Chris is making an effort to learn a little of the language, 'though not for any jingoistic reason'. He just thinks that he would like to be able to have a modest conversation or exchange civilities on the occasions that he is in the company of Irish-language speakers.

He is particularly impressed by Linda Ervine, a former communist from east Belfast who took up the study of Irish in adult life and now runs an Irish-language development project called Turas in a largely Protestant part of Belfast. Linda told me, 'I wish I had known twenty years ago that I could just go and learn this. There is a sense within a Protestant community that this is something that Catholics do and we don't.'

And she says she felt an immediate attraction to Irish: 'Is it, as somebody once said to me, that without knowing it, it is in us because it is all around us and is the language of our ancestry and place names. Something naturally draws us to it. I can't answer that but I know for me there just was this overwhelming desire to get this language.'

Perhaps it is that sense of natural affinity that Fintan O'Toole overlooked when he suggested that people are merely 'virtue signalling' when they claim to love the language and tell census collectors that they speak it and yet never use it in their lives.

Neale Richmond, who learned Irish at school, is now trying to learn it again:

I get awful stick, like all the new TDs taking Irish classes because they think they are going to be whatever in the future.

I had to give a speech last week in a gaelscoil and it was right beside the estate where I grew up. I have never been so nervous in my life for a thirty-second speech. And again, my best canvasser during an election – she didn't teach me any Irish because I wasn't good enough in school – was head of Irish in my school and she was married to a clergyman from a very prominent Church of Ireland family in Tipperary, so that's why I think there's an awful lot of contradiction.

In my constituency we have opened three gaelscoils and a gael coláiste in the last decade. The Irish language is growing and it is seen not necessarily in a nationalist sort of way.

Sixty per cent of people interviewed for an RTÉ TG4 survey said that Irish was very important to them, but nearly 70 per cent of them said they never spoke it at all.

The language is deployed tokenistically in political party names, official titles like Taoiseach and Ceann Comhairle, in signing off the weather forecast on RTÉ or in the first paragraph of public speeches. So the language has become a focus of national reverence more than an actual medium for the passage of information.

That is not what was planned by the founders of the Irish nation. They believed that Ireland would not have established itself as free and independent until Irish was the language spoken by ordinary people on the bus, in the workplace, in the pub and in the home. They thought that the first generation of children compulsorily taught through Irish in primary schools would grow up to be an adult population speaking it in every part of their lives, but it didn't work.

Instead, the political and cultural efforts to revive Irish incentivised people to claim a greater facility with it than they actually had. In Northern Ireland political republicans and language campaigners have urged people to say on census forms that they speak Irish. And this can seem like a generous and responsible thing to do because it can reinforce an argument for the funding of Irish-language projects. It can help the language along and it's not strictly a lie if you can say, 'Cad é mar atá tú?'

But what is the impact on a community of living with the lie that it is more Gaelic than it really is? In her book *Saints, Scholars and Schizophrenics*, written in the 1970s, Nancy Scheper-Hughes claims that the strain of this pretence is demoralising. The promotion of the gaeltacht areas was intended to revitalise those areas but instead produced huge discouragement.

Scheper-Hughes wrote that, 'Leaders of the [Irish language] movement … concentrated on the symbolic importance of the language as containing the very soul of the Irish people.' To illustrate this concept, she quotes a government pamphlet defending compulsory Irish-language education: 'The Irish language is the expression of our personality as a nation, or our identity, of our pride in being ourselves.' Something of that sense also resonates in what Linda Ervine said, but a possible corollary of it is the message that you are not really Irish at all if you don't cherish the language.

The misfortune for those who wished to revive the language, Scheper-Hughes argues, is that it was already 'moribund' by the time their campaign started. She conducted her research in An Clochan in Kerry, at a time when it was recovering its lost status as a Gaeltacht and thereby attracting funding.

When she arrived as a researcher she heard a lot of Irish spoken and even apologised to interviewees for addressing them in English, though they all spoke English well. She discovered that, after the first enthusiasm, the use of Irish around her waned and that failure to keep up the Irish was an embarrassment. '[Some] villagers protested that the Irish revival movement and Gaeltacht status had made liars of the whole community.'

They had been speaking Irish in the presence of outsiders for fear that they were government inspectors. She tells of a public health nurse being denied access to a home because the woman answering the door felt that she had to pretend that she didn't understand the visitor's English.

In an introduction to a later edition of her book, Scheper-Hughes revealed that she had been criticised by villagers for her claim that their Irish speaking was a charade and was told that when a new priest came and led prayers in English many in the pews would respond in Irish.

While the Republic has learned that making Irish a 'first official language' has not succeeded in making its use general and, in fact, has alienated many of its own people, not exclusively Protestants, Northern Ireland is now moving to make Irish an official language there, which can be used in the government documentation and in the courts where speaking in Irish has been banned since 1737.

The government is adapting to the use of Irish as a communications medium, for which it is not needed. I doubt that a single person in Northern Ireland speaks Irish better than English. The language serves as an icon of Irish identity and facilitation of the language stands for respect for that Irish identity. But nobody actually needs government documents translated into Irish in order to be better able to understand them.

As early as the 1950s, Hubert Butler, in 'Portrait of a Minority', said that compulsory Irish in the Republic had become 'a cynical travesty'. Even so, both North and South are now legislating for promotion of the Irish language in public services and government. Recently the Irish government updated the Official Languages Act 2003 to commit the government to ensuring that at least 20 per cent of the staff of public bodies will be proficient in Irish by 2030. This has implications for Irish unity because many in Northern Ireland who don't use Irish – that is, nearly everyone – might feel much less inclined to vote for a united Ireland if they fear that they would be excluding themselves from 20 per cent of public service jobs.

It will be interesting to see how many native English speakers in Northern Ireland will exercise their new right to insist on their court cases being heard in Irish. If they do, they will largely be speaking through translators who speak English no better than they do themselves. Will anyone risk the outcome of a court case on the insistence of arguing a legal case in a language the judge and jury probably won't understand when they can as easily, or more easily, deliver it in one they do?

For three years, until 2020, Sinn Féin refused to enter government in Northern Ireland and restore a collapsed executive until unionists agreed to an Irish Language Act which would make Irish an official language of the state. That's how important this has been to them. Their attitude echoes a claim by de Valera that he would prioritise the language over Irish independence, since independence could be secured later, but if the language was allowed to die out it would never recover.

Neither government appears daunted by past failure in efforts to stimulate official use of Irish, nor have they seriously considered whether promoting it in official documents is the best way to revive the vernacular. The English that people speak is not the English of parliamentary bills and reports. A few good songs would probably have more effect.

De Valera's project was not so much about helping people to love the language as about attaching a sense of patriotic duty to it. One of the most respected Irish-language campaigners and writers, Séamus Ó Grianna, a native speaker from Ranafast in Donegal, ultimately argued against the teaching of Irish in Gaeltacht schools because the new formalised language was a modern invention and anyway, since the people were still migrating for work, English would be of more use to them.

At a discussion on the prospects of a united Ireland in the Mansion House in Dublin in November 2021, a member of the audience asked the Sinn Féin president, Mary Lou McDonald, if, in a united Ireland, compulsory Irish education would be imposed on the people of east Belfast. She had argued for harmonisation of laws north and south to make unification simpler.

McDonald said, 'We shouldn't make it mandatory in east Belfast and we don't have to because they are voting with their feet and with their fáinne óir. And I want to commend Linda Ervine for the incredible work she has done, a loyalist woman to her roots.' She got warm applause for this from people with as little understanding of east Belfast as she has herself, though presumably not making Irish instruction mandatory there after unification would undermine the current laws by which it is mandatory in the rest of Ireland.

And she misrepresented Linda Ervine, who was never a loyalist. Her family were communists. Her father was a member of the executive of the Northern Ireland Civil Rights Association and she spent much of her childhood in Twinbrook, a predominantly Catholic housing estate in west Belfast. Presenting her to a Dublin audience as evidence that solid loyalists can be won over isn't fair to her or to that audience.

No such evidence exists. We are not going to ground a future all-Ireland identity on the Irish language, and trying to do that is likely to alienate not only unionists but also those of us who may value Irish as a symbol of identity but are not going to put in the hard work of learning to use it.

8

THE STORIES WE TELL OURSELVES

MY FATHER AND mother lived in an Ireland which was culturally almost uniform. Gays and pregnant young women hid themselves away or were shunned and imprisoned. We could watch RTÉ television with a special aerial, two BBC channels and UTV. We could listen to a small range of BBC radio stations as well as Radio Éireann broadcasting from Athlone.

As young teenagers in Northern Ireland, we could tune into Radio Luxembourg on a Sunday night to hear whining interference and ads for Elida along with the latest music from Marty Wilde and Tommy Steele. The media available to us, shaping our tastes and feeding them, expanded rapidly with every new station that came along. We could get what books we wanted, even if in the Republic they were censored, and we could see most new popular films too. But still there was something like a national conversation.

We didn't need water cooler moments, for which an event has to be so exceptionally interesting as to break through the general media hubbub. In the 1960s and 1970s we talked about the television we had all watched the night before and the latest album by Simon and Garfunkel.

The internet has transformed the media landscape completely. People can now pass whole days amusing themselves with YouTube or porn sites or reading the *Hindustan Times* or *The Boston Globe*. They can book a weekend trip to Budapest on a cheap deal and walk round their hotel or survey the city from the air before leaving home.

So, if a nation is an agreed imagined community, with a sense of there being standards and interests to conform to, what is left today that is uniform about Ireland?

Well, quite a lot.

In the mid-seventies, I lived for a time in India. I returned there in 2019, after forty years. By then the population had doubled and the bright sky I had known had been turned beige by pollution. No one under forty had been born in the India I had known, when there were only two Indian-built makes of car on the roads. The country was changed utterly. In the mornings I had watched a river of bicycles on the ring road pass my front gate, along with cycle rickshaws and tongas, little horse-drawn traps like the ones called jaunting cars on Irish postcards. Now they are gone, driven off the expanded ring road by the chaos of horn-beeping cars.

And yet, something was still obviously India, in about the same balance of enchanting and exasperating that I had known before.

An American cousin who had come here in the 1970s and then returned today would not find anything like the same degree of change, would know us as Irish people in our manners and interests, but would probably note the drop-off in church attendance, remembering how, when passing a Catholic church on a Sunday morning in Westport or Ballycastle, you'd see worshippers kneeling on the steps trying to follow the ritual inside.

In India I met young women with short hair, dressed in jeans and shirts who talked of their plans to study in America. Forty years earlier they would have adhered to the tradition of long hair, baggy pants and frock top and stole.

The surprise in Ireland might be same sex couples walking hand-in-hand through Dublin or Belfast, but many of those changes have happened in other countries and are not distinctly Irish, like the crowds outside the pubs smoking, the people studying their phones as they walk past, the electric scooters, the cycle lanes. From gay rights and abortion rights to the promotion of cycling and the disdain for smoking, Ireland has changed in conformity with international standards, not in response to some indigenous spirit or character.

When I reflect on Indian ways, risking the charge that I am superficial or worse, racist, the little things I notice, and that other visitors to India comment on, are how people on meeting me will seek to assess me or will invite me to their homes to impose food on me. The taxi driver from the airport immediately wants to know how many cars and children I have.

If I was looking for some Irish characteristic or trait, what might it be? How we comment on the weather when we meet? How drivers in the countryside raise a finger off the steering wheel or tilt the head to greet a driver coming the other way? Do these things still describe us? I'm not sure.

I am sitting in my dining room, writing at the table on a laptop and looking around me and wondering how anyone, if shown a photograph of me in my immediate surroundings, would know I was in Ireland. Once this room was surfaced over compacted soil with little red and black tiles. There was probably a range. But the old fireplace is now sealed up and stacked with books. Even they don't denote Ireland. What catches my eye in a quick glance to my right is Kazuo Ishiguro, Robert Graves and Karl Ove Knausgård. Yes, there are Banvilles and Rooneys here, but probably not in a greater proportion than you'd find in a similar room in Manchester.

There are paintings and prints on the walls by artists from Iceland and Ukraine, and Ireland as well, of course. The biggest giveaway that this is Ireland would be the traditional dresser stacked with Kilkenny pottery that my wife loves and collects, but you can buy that in Boston and Berlin too, and no doubt it has its adherents there.

So what makes this space Ireland and makes me Irish?

Quite a lot. The way I use the language, the humour that people around me share and which becomes less intelligible and less funny the further I move from home. But like everyone else here, I have an international dimension to my thinking and culture that could not have been conceived of by my parents. Which must mean that my Irishness, the part of me that is Irish and thinks in Irish ways, has shrunk.

A small exception to this change is my mother-in-law, who doesn't use a computer or mobile phone and doesn't think she needs one. Yet she gets me to set up an iPad to let her watch Mass in the local church through its webcam when she is unwell.

That generation which hasn't been able to adapt to the technology of the internet will die out and be replaced soon with old people who would be lost without it. The phenomenon of a generational divide between the cyber-sussed and those with analogue brains will be no more.

The founders of the Irish nation were determined that Ireland would be different from Britain, above the filthy modern tide. We can only suppose that if the ghosts of Pearse and de Valera walked among us today they would be appalled.

*

We ask if Ireland can be one. Can any country be one?

The historian Benedict Anderson, in his book *Imagined Communities*, theorises about the emergence of nations and, along the way, cites several examples of what draws people together into a shared national identity and sense of purpose. One is a literature which represents and addresses a community of people who are expected to understand and empathise with the characters. A good example of this would be Sally Rooney's *Normal People*, which speaks to a secular Irish generation. In the normality of the lives of young lovers there is no reference to the Church or even to a generational disdain for their sexual freedom. The book would have been banned in an earlier Ireland, but actually it is inconceivable that it could even have been written, so abnormal would the lives of Connell and Marianne have been in that context.

There is a northern story which southern people express little interest in. And there is a southern story which northerners, whether nationalist or unionist, are out of touch with. As a writer from Belfast, I have addressed more literary festivals in Scotland than in the Irish Republic. Even where festivals in Dublin or Dún Laoghaire feature northern writers, they specifically identify them as such. So Michael Longley and Sinead Morrissey win prizes and read to large audiences, but they do so on a presumption that they are from elsewhere, that they are acknowledged to have taken great trouble to come, that they speak out of an experience which is remote. Similarly, Irish writers who come north may receive warm welcomes and long queues for signings, but they are seen as almost exotic beings, certainly as speaking into issues which are not quite ours.

Some writers from Northern Ireland have been taken in as one of their own by the people of the Republic but not many. Seamus Heaney crossed the border in both senses. He moved to Dublin and he won love and admiration there and across the world. A few others have also managed this. Jan Carson may be one.

Jan is a Northern Irish novelist who grew up in an evangelical Christian culture. Her most recent novel, *The Raptures*, is set in a small Protestant town in Northern Ireland among conservative believers and a diverse range of bigots, chauvinists and generally small-minded rural people wrestling with the mystery that their children are dying. She says she has been more welcome in the south of Ireland than in England:

> When I have been down to far-flung places like Listowel and west Cork there is a general lack of understanding about Protestant, particularly unionist culture, but it is not ignorance in the way we say ignorance in Northern Ireland, it's genuine ignorance. They just don't know and they want to learn.
>
> They are curious in a nice healthy way. It makes me sad that we couldn't have had those conversations thirty or forty years ago. Two people come up to you in a bar

and say, here now, what is an Orangeman, can you explain it to me? I am completely happy to do that. It's done with no malice.

Whereas what I often get in English festivals is a sense that they do understand and they are going to tell you that they understand.

She feels that her sense of being British is diminished when Britain fails to notice or take account of Northern Ireland: 'It makes me so angry when I hear the BBC news listing the pandemic numbers for Scotland, Wales and England and not mentioning us. It feels like you're not wanted and I have had such a rich welcome from the Irish contingent – it's a very natural thing to go where you are wanted.'

However, she does reflect cynically on the sometimes warm Irish response to her. Southerners perhaps congratulate themselves on getting on with a northern Protestant without really having made contact with a passionate unionist. 'I'm an easy person to include as somebody from a traditional unionist background but who is willing to have these conversations. It allows them to say, look we are engaging with Protestant northerners.'

The writers she names as ones she has a close affinity with are other northern Protestants: Wendy Erskine and Glenn Patterson, suggesting that she is more northern than Irish. 'I can see that I am a Protestant writer, but I would hate it if I was solely a Protestant writer and solely beloved of that community. That would be horrific.'

I quote to her the remark about the Catholics doing the writing and the Protestants inventing the tractor. She says:

Some of my story is of growing up conservative Presbyterian and having to push through that theological barrier into the arts. One of the things I have really enjoyed about being an Irish writer is loosening up a bit. I feel that from the southern writers I have learned how to let my hair down, how to be much more free in my storytelling and to laugh at myself. That has been a great thing. In my early experiences with writing, I was so uptight and earnest and very serious all the time.

She has emerged from a culture she describes as dour and insular, wary of Catholic neighbours, which had no sense of having anything to learn from Catholics. Yet the modern literature that she engaged with did often reflect the Catholic world and the Irish experience. It had much less to say about the closed evangelical culture which she describes in her work:

> Growing up there was such a lot of art about the Catholic experience. I didn't set foot in a chapel until I was twenty-two, but I could have told you a lot about what was going on in the Mass and what a Catholic funeral or wedding was like because it was conveyed in literature and film, but it is not there from the Protestant side so there is a curiosity.

Jan is surprised by the ease with which some people assume that a united Ireland is inevitable:

> People come up from time to time to work out what the mood is in Northern Ireland and they talk to the obvious

suspects and they never go and talk to people like my parents who belong to a rural Presbyterian church. They have just as much right to be heard and to have an influence on what happens in the future.

She says that art is supposed to be 'the canary in the coal mine', the early indicator of change, but there is no indication breaking through in the arts of an enthusiasm for a united Ireland:

> A united Ireland wouldn't be a calamity. I think like a lot of people, I am afraid of how we get to that point. The repercussions and the tensions. I think that in some ways the Good Friday Agreement is the ultimate suspension of disbelief. It doesn't really work. There is no way of fixing Northern Ireland and making it satisfying to everyone. And we have just kept believing and suspending disbelief in this thing that kind of works. I would be quite happy to continue being part of the UK or to be part of a wider united Ireland if I could continue to have the life and the opportunity and the prospects that I enjoy and want for my family and my niece and nephew.

Jan writes out of a community but not exclusively for that community. To be seen in such a way, she says would horrify her. Apart from the community she emerged from is the community of writers she merges into, and that community is Irish. So she is playing her part in constructing an Irish cultural identity which includes and appreciates northern Protestants.

*

Benedict Anderson, who wrote about how communities are imagined into existence, describes the artform that is the novel as binding people together, but he says that, in like fashion, the newspaper achieves the same but more rapidly, more extensively. Yet if you want to buy the *Belfast Telegraph* in Dublin you will have some difficulty finding it. And although *The Irish Times* and the *Irish Independent* are sold in Belfast, the big tabloids have their separate editions and now the *Sunday Independent* has a northern edition. The intention behind this may be to enlarge a national conversation, but surely the way to do that would be to ensure that all parts of the country were receiving the same paper.

And anyway, newspaper sales are plummeting. If Anderson were writing today, he would also have to consider the wider proliferation of TV channels after digitalisation, as well as the spread of social media.

When there was only one station, in my early youth, the whole country watched the same news programmes at the same time. Newsreaders like Richard Baker and Robert Dougal on the BBC presented an air of sober authority, setting the national mood, deciding for us what was important to know. Now you can go through life without watching the news at all or relying on a channel which accords with your taste and interests and disregarding the rest.

There is a curious phenomenon, however, that a consumer's market in television somehow draws strong audiences to Netflix and to the most popular shows and films on it. Generally, social media leads to the fragmentation of the imagined community into smaller, more focused communities of interest.

I can't imagine that if we still had just one channel and the modest authority of Richard Baker to keep us in line

that there would have been such dissent from good sense in
response to the coronavirus, including the fact that, going by
northern figures, one in five health service workers refused to
be vaccinated. Eccentric positions now have their platforms and
the most startling by-product of that has been the populism
which brought Donald Trump to the US presidency and enabled
English nationalism to revolt against the European Union.

How important is the state in all this?

How much attention is any populace now paying to its
government?

Anderson also included the commemoration of war as
a major binding influence in the reinforcement of national
identity. After the Second World War, numerous films celebrated
the great British achievement of curtailing the advance of the
Hun with a little help from America. Rarely was anything said
about Stalin's Russia having been an ally. However, when you
endorse your status today with reference to past wars, you have
to edit whopping contradictions out of those stories.

The TV westerns of my childhood years depicted native
Americans as savage 'injuns'. Even today the British do not
want to look frankly at the mass incineration of German
civilians during the Second World War. That war has been
mythologised as a time when the nation held together under
threat of annihilation. Pride in being British was validated by
that collective experience. It was a timely opportunity to rebind
the nation when the other great source of pride, the Empire,
was withering away.

But what war could the new Irish look back to as unifying
them, as marking the high point of collective endeavour and
national resilience?

For northern unionists, the First World War is more important in their mythology than the Second. Their young were slaughtered at the Somme and on the other battlefields in France and Belgium. They are not remembered as squandered cannon fodder but as noble people who made a profound sacrifice that warrants repaying. And what were those sneaky Irish up to at the same time? Well, in fact, many of them were being strafed to bits in no man's land too, but unionists best remember the ones in Dublin who stabbed the country in the back and turned fire on the very army that was fighting for everyone's freedom. That's how they see it.

The Troubles in the North are remembered in ways that endorse imagined communities too. Sinn Féin preserves the legacy of the Provisional IRA and endorses its murderous campaign as a legitimate struggle against occupation, although perhaps it is softening on this. Mary Lou McDonald, speaking at that Mansion House discussion organised by Ireland's Future, was interesting in her statement that it was 'not my job' to hand down a prescription of what sort of country a united Ireland should be. In the republican tradition it was very much the job of Sinn Féin to preserve a vision of a free Ireland as imagined in the Proclamation. The Provisional movement took its name from the provisional government declared by Patrick Pearse at the GPO.

Perhaps the contradiction of celebrating an insular Catholic Gael as your leader and inspiration while seeking to unite Ireland as culturally diverse inside the European Union is presenting some difficulty.

The war that northern republicans bond together to commemorate is the IRA campaign from the 1970s. They are not going to concede that that campaign was wrong-headed and destructive. They are not going to undermine their legendary martyrs. Ultimately, in the new Ireland, they will want statues to Bobby Sands and Martin McGuinness, or railway stations or roads named after them, so that it will be no more acceptable to scoff at them than to scoff at James Connolly or Michael Collins. They already have their memorials in the North, their murals and plaques, just as the loyalists have theirs. They have their anniversaries, rituals and icons.

For the Republic, it is the War of Independence that it chooses to commemorate. It has its heroes from that conflict, but so far it is loath to include anyone who died for Ireland after 1922. So the commemoration of war is not going to be a binding force for the creation of a coherent Irish nation.

Nor will religion or language.

9

NATIONALISM

NEARLY HALF THE people in Northern Ireland are loosely described as nationalists. They are not really nationalists. A few are perhaps. The mistake has been made before that all of these people, at least those of voting age and above, want a united Ireland.

In the early days of the Northern Ireland Troubles, then Taoiseach Jack Lynch argued in a summit with the British Prime Minister Ted Heath that all of 'the minority' in Northern Ireland wanted out of the UK and rid of the border. He didn't use the word 'nationalists'. It had not come into common currency yet but was settled on later by general agreement as an adequate descriptor of people who previously have been called the minority or the Catholics.

Heath doubted Lynch's claim and called a border poll, which was inconclusive because the people called 'the minority' declined to vote. The more republican-minded among their leaders probably did not want the embarrassment of an outcome that did not affirm their claims and thereby diminished their influence. As it turned out, after another twenty-six years, the main political leadership of these people – whatever we are to call them – settled for the compromise of the Good Friday

Agreement in 1998, which put unity where they wanted it, in the future.

We call them nationalists, not because they necessarily evince the characteristics of nationalists in other parts of the world, as observed or defined by academics who have written on the subject, but because we can't call them Catholics any more. Even unionists and the British were wary of calling them Catholics when the Troubles started. Most of those, in fact nearly all of those, who vote for parties which say they want a united Ireland, were indeed baptised Catholic or were born of parents who were baptised Catholic. But if they are not actually practising Catholic worship or expressing any theological convictions through their politics, their being of Catholic extraction could not be the most pertinent fact about them.

That it may be a predictor of how they will vote is inconvenient. That fact nudges us back into recognising what a handy term Catholic is. We can substitute it for person who is unlikely to vote for any unionist party and more likely to vote Sinn Féin, SDLP, Alliance or for the Green Party. It is never going to be an exact label. It is essentially code or shorthand, a generalisation which can sometimes help clarify things and at other times obscures reality.

Is it not unfair to actual believing Catholics to retain their designation beyond its appropriateness just because it is a handy label for a bunch of people we would like to lump together as not-unionist? What should we then call actual believing Catholics to distinguish them from the others we have chosen to call Catholic for convenience?

Using labels beyond their literal meaning can lead us to

preserve in language the myth of coherence in a community which is actually fragmenting. At what point would we give up the label or find ourselves dragging out a mythical community categorisation to the extent that we were losing touch with how things actually are? I have already accused Brendan O'Leary in Chapter One of doing that when he described Stephen Farry of the Alliance Party as a 'cultural Catholic'.

There are other words, like 'fenian' and 'taig', 'popehead', 'papist'. These are always deployed as insults, though they are occasionally incorporated into humour that parodies sectarian attitudes. I like 'taig', though I have been rebuked for using it on radio. It has the merit of being virtually meaningless. The words 'fenian' and 'papist' attribute ideologies to people, which they may not actually hold. In that sense they disguise sectarianism as a political or religious dispute. The word 'taig' is a more honest expression of contempt for me as Irish, regardless of what I actually believe. It lets me know where I stand. It confronts me with honest bigotry. It is the Irish word for Tim, or a perversion of it. Glasgow Celtic supporters call themselves the Tims. If someone calls me a taig I know what they mean. They mean that I am Irish and thereby distinct from others who are not Irish. This is what this labelling is all about; determining boundaries between communities where precise boundaries cannot be found. If they could be found, we would have labels that we could apply to them.

We who are the taigs don't want the non-taigs, the prods, whatever, to call us Irish, because that would imply that they are not Irish themselves. We want them to think that they are Irish too. Irish is a nice broad word that no longer presumes that one is Catholic or nationalist. In the Republic it need not be taken to represent anything other than nationality or lineage. You could never say that one was less Irish because of religion or politics, that voting for one party or attending a Zen monastery or a Presbyterian church makes that person less Irish than if they voted Fianna Fáil and went to Mass in the cathedral every morning. So if we use the word Irish to label the people formerly known as the Catholics or the nationalists, we deny it to others, some of whom may want to apply it to themselves.

There is no polite word for the Irish-identifying people of Northern Ireland that does not presume that they believe things that they might not believe, but the word which most of the media and political culture has settled on is nationalist. It is a label that both unionists and nationalists agree on in a region in which many names and labels are contested.

My obituary, if I warrant one, will most likely say that I grew up in a nationalist community. It's not true. For a start, what is the community? Is it the housing estate or the constituency, inclusive of people I don't even know, or just my neighbours? Who decided the parameters of my community, let alone attributed political attitudes to it?

The constituency returns representatives of nationalist parties, but not everybody votes and some vote for other parties. People are thrown up by other groupings and declared to be community representatives, though unelected. They say they have their finger on the pulse of the community, that they know by some deeper intuition what the community really wants. Others may vote for nationalist parties without being nationalists themselves.

Ian Dunt, in his book *How To Be A Liberal*, starts off by defining nationalism. Interestingly he says that it is spreading across the world and that nowhere is immune to its advance, yet he doesn't include Ireland in his list of the most worrying manifestations of what he clearly sees as an undesirable political ambition. We lightly call ourselves or others nationalists in Northern Ireland, yet theorists of nationalism can't fit us into their theories. What we have is something else.

Nationalism, Dunt says, is built on six lies. The first is that you do not exist as an individual.

There is something of that in the determination to designate whole communities as nationalist. None of the political representatives of those communities would say outright that you are obliged by birth or residence to endorse a nationalist ideology, but you can pick that attitude up on the social media of those who bat for the republican cause. If you have an Irish name like mine and went to a Catholic school as I did, but you contest a core principle like, for instance, the unfortunate inevitability of the Provisional IRA, then they have a ready barrage of epithets for you. You are a souper, a West Brit, a turncoat, an Uncle Tom.

Similarly loyalists of the 'any taig will do' attitude have been content to kill random Catholics and trust that they were striking back at the IRA. It was of no concern whether the 'taig' was an atheist, a Rastafarian or campaigned for the Alliance Party.

But how extensive is that toxic thinking and how active within our political discourse?

It is there, perhaps, but it is shamefaced and anonymous. Party members who get caught out having tweeted sectarian or sexist comments are rebuked or sacked, but anonymous party supporters spew such filth constantly, suggesting that those attitudes are actually engrained. That alone tells you something. In some other countries downright bigots declare themselves, like the Hindus disrupting Muslim worship in the middle-class areas of Delhi.

Ian Dunt says that the second lie of the nationalist is that the world is simple.

I could easily accuse Irish republicans of holding that belief. Despite the lesson we learned from the Brexit referendum, that a simple yes/no question can lead you into conflict and turmoil, there are still those who want an early border poll on a straightforward 'unity or not' question, to be decided on a simple majority of 50 per cent plus one of those who vote. That indeed is what the Good Friday Agreement prescribes at a time when the British Secretary of State determines that the vote may be carried. But many others understand that there has to be considerable preparation before a vote, probably with Citizen's Assemblies deciding what the question should be and what form unity should take.

The question here is whether the majority of people believe unity relies on a simple question, easily resolved and implemented. I don't think they do. That some might be so politically reckless as try to bounce us into a vote is possible, of course.

Sinn Féin and other groups argue that Irish unity is inevitable. That is simplistic thinking, but even they are urging unionists to come into the discussion, perhaps to make the debate more credible, but perhaps also on the understanding that some complexities will have to be dealt with.

The third lie that Dunt has identified from the conduct of nationalist movements around the world is that you must not question.

Sinn Féin has been fairly abrupt in its dealing with those who have had difficulty accepting the party's democratic centralism. Candidates selected by constituencies have been replaced at short notice on orders from above. But to focus more broadly on the people who are called 'nationalists' – for that is the word we are scrutinising – they are not homogenous and averse to discussion. Many vote for the SDLP or the Alliance Party. Though whole populations of housing estates get called 'nationalist', some there don't vote at all, some don't get out of bed and some keep pigeons. The people of, say, Twinbrook in west Belfast are as diverse as the people of Tallaght, some of whom are Zen Buddhists and have more important questions on their minds than whether an island should be a single jurisdiction. And if this island, why not the island next door?

Dunt's fourth identified lie is that the institutions of state are conspiring against the people.

I think a lot of people in what we call the nationalist communities in the North do believe that. But do they believe it deeply? They certainly think that their government will hoodwink them and cheat them out of welfare benefits and pretend to be reinforcing the health service while depleting it. But do they believe that the police officer who stops their car to breathalyse them in the week before Christmas will fake the result to create an excuse to arrest them? I don't think they do. They are cynical about politics, but most don't live with the assumption that the state is a perpetual enemy, although some do, of course.

We have seen throughout the Covid-19 pandemic that some people clearly believe that the pandemic is fake and that several governments around the world are complicit in a plot to manipulate their populations. In Ireland there is no immediate association between that belief and Irish nationalism, though republican flags have been waved at anti-vaccine protests. Graffiti claiming that the virus is a hoax has appeared on both the unionist Shankill and the nationalist Falls areas of Belfast.

The fifth lie which Dunt lists is that difference is bad.

Nationalists in other countries are suspicious of gays, Muslims, people of a different colour or sexual orientation. This does not apply to the so-called nationalist communities of Northern Ireland. Davy Adams, who was a loyalist activist, says he recognises that nationalism in Ireland is different from racist forms of it elsewhere:

> You only have to look beyond these shores, and sometimes not too far distant, at the leaderships thrown up in other countries to realise that things in Ireland could be an awful lot worse. There are massively important distinctions between those leaderships and Sinn Féin. Despite their faults, to their credit the Shinners have never been racist, nor have they ever opposed immigration, or the acceptance into the country of refugees.

If anything, most people in those communities express liberal and tolerant ideas. Now, one may cynically argue that they do so in order to distinguish themselves from unionists who, they perceive, are illiberal and racist. Or maybe they do so in order to identify themselves with the secularising and liberalising tendencies in the Republic, to ride that wave. But, as Dunt illustrates, real nationalists, as defined by him, are not ashamed to express their bigotry proudly and very little of that attitude is manifest in the political voices of those in Northern Ireland whom we define as nationalist.

Lie number six told by real nationalists, he says, is that there is no such thing as truth: 'Evidence and reason, the qualities that allow humanity to aspire towards certainty, are dismissed as plots against the people.' (Dunt, 2020, p. 10.)

We heard that lie during the Brexit debates, the exasperation with experts. We hear it from anti-vaxxers. We get some of it in Irish nationalism in the dismissal of some history as 'revisionist'. By this view there is a clear and simple narrative of Irish experience under oppression and no one has the right to undermine that story. Evidence which qualifies that story will be ignored or reviled.

That has indeed been part of our experience, but whether that contempt for evidence is a characteristic of the community we call nationalist is another matter, and I would say it isn't, though it is certainly voiced by some within it.

Can the same test be applied to unionists? Are they nationalists of a kind by Dunt's definition?

Matthew O'Toole, who sits on the New Ireland Commission established by the SDLP in Northern Ireland, says, 'The word nationalist has become associated with a type of exclusivist politics which is on the increase around Europe. A lot of unionists are more nationalist in that sense than I am. My use of the word nationalist only describes my constitutional preference. It doesn't describe my politics.'

Unionists, as Protestants, do very much argue that you exist as an individual. That deals with Lie 1, that you don't. But there certainly are strands of thought among unionists that the world is very simple (Lie 2), for instance, that it was created in six days by God 6,000 years ago. There doesn't seem to be the same determination among Catholics to take the Bible literally. The world for a Protestant evangelical is, therefore, much simpler than science attests, for their theology dismisses evolution, geology, astronomy and, by inference, the speed of light.

I don't think that as a community or ideology they forbid questioning (Lie 3), though you are not a unionist if you don't believe in the Union, so I suppose they are nationalists by that part of the definition; British nationalists of course. No unionist politician who spoke in favour of ending the Union would remain within the fold. Yet all who endorse the Good Friday Agreement accept that the Union is subject to a democratic vote, so the old theologically grounded dogmatic unionism of Ian Paisley is now obsolete.

Do they think the institutions of the state are conspiring against them (Lie 4)? Indeed, many do. They believe that Britain has a long-term plan for dumping Northern Ireland and that they must be vigilant against this happening. But this may not actually be a lie and therefore would not fit into Dunt's theory.

Do unionists believe that difference is bad (Lie 5)? Many certainly do. They recruit for their parties and canvass for votes almost exclusively among people who are usually called Protestants, though this is no more accurate a label for them than Catholic is for the so-called nationalists.

The most concerted effort of a unionist party to extend itself beyond its traditional community parameters was the

campaign of the UUP led by Doug Beattie to present a more
secular and liberal agenda. Doug was never in the Orange Order
and doesn't go to church, so is hardly even really a Protestant.
He says:

> I guess those people who are coming up in the middle
> are saying, I don't want that negative pessimistic unionist
> message that's going out at this time. I want something
> different. So if you are not able to reach out and give
> them something more positive you will lose them, and
> unionism will just wither and die on the vine and that's
> just the way it's going to be.

Doug is an army veteran who fought in Afghanistan and
actually killed a man with a bayonet in close combat. That army
experience and respect for the British military tradition can
endear him to traditionalist unionists though his secularism
tends to alienate many of them. He says:

> If you are sitting in political unionism now and you
> think that the core vote which is a Protestant community
> core vote is going to sustain us in the coming years,
> then you are far mistaken. The young people coming
> up who still identify as being Protestant, or maybe not
> identifying, are looking for a different future. And the
> different future isn't that negative pessimistic politics
> that political unionism is promoting now. And they
> look at it and they are turned off it straight away and
> they go elsewhere.

Unionism is, however, still suffused with actual believing Protestantism in a way that nationalism is no longer suffused with theological Catholicism. Even so, Doug Beattie's party rallied round to preserve his leadership when the country was scandalised by the disclosure of smutty and sexist tweets he had posted years before he became party leader.

Nationalists do not, as a condition of being nationalist, revere the Pope, though some unionists think that the way to insult all nationalists is to write 'Fuck the Pope' on walls. This only offends because the intention behind it is clear. Most people in those areas would probably have no greater day-to-day concern for the welfare of the Pope than for that of Bono, but writing 'Fuck Bono' on the walls would not be understood by them as an affront.

Unionists evince a greater reverence for the Queen than so-called nationalists do for the Pope. In the original wars of the sixteenth century, the Pope and the British monarch were prime icons of opposing sides. That has changed to the extent that what so-called nationalists think of the Pope tells us nothing about whether or not they want a united Ireland.

As for the idea that unionists might believe that there is no such thing as truth (Lie 6), it's complicated. Many do believe in the absolute truth of the Bible and therefore reject all authority or scientific finding – as in evolution or astronomy – which contradicts it. But you don't get expelled from unionism for believing that there are visible stars and galaxies more than 6,000 light years away from us or that the farmyard cockerel is a descendent of Tyrannosaurus Rex.

Ostensibly the only qualification for being a de facto unionist is that you believe that Northern Ireland should stay part of the United Kingdom. However, unionist political culture is so focused on monarchy and so reverential of the imperial tradition and the Protestant faith that it appears to be inseparable from them.

So unionism is a form of nationalism, though a moderate one by Dunt's definition, in that it concedes that it can be defeated by a majority vote for Irish unity.

In the past, unionism has been highly cultural and thereby excluded many who might agree on the one fundamental of staying in the UK. However, some sections of unionism are changing. For instance, Mervyn Gibson, Grand Secretary of the Orange Order, says he now explains to Orangemen and unionists that to defend the Union they have to seek allegiances with people who may have different moral values from their own. He understands that the future is with those who are not nationalists, either British or Irish, but with the middle ground who will make the pragmatic decision. Mervyn says:

> Traditionally it would have been the Protestant community that supported the Union. And you can trace that back to when Roman Catholics were barred from holding office in the military and all sorts of things in the 1700s. But society has changed. I think Northern Ireland showed that you didn't have to be a Protestant to be a unionist and indeed many high positions within the government and the civil service and the police force were held by Roman Catholics. So it wasn't intrinsically a Protestant state in the terms it is frequently accused of nowadays, but it was strongly Protestant in character.

In effect, he accepts that Northern Ireland can no longer be defined as Protestant. At the same time he wants to refute the allegation that it was ever sectarian:

> I don't think it was inherently or deliberately sectarian. Did sectarian things happen? Of course they did. They happened down south too. They were of their day. Today you can be a unionist and be a whole lot of things that probably wouldn't have been seen as unionist in the past. No longer is the Union safe just by saying we are Protestant and we are unionist and Orange and it will stay that way.

Some envisage a new Ireland which would be enriched by diversity rather than torn apart by differences over identity. Matthew O'Toole of the New Ireland Commission says:

> I want a definition of Ireland and Irishness which is genuinely and truly inclusive, inclusive to the extent that it celebrates everything on this island. And that has produced a huge amount of angst, anger and anxiety. I think creating an Ireland which is genuinely pluralist and genuinely inclusive of every tradition and allegiance on this island is something worth aspiring to.

It's the sort of thing Neale Richmond might say.

Both might be intrigued by Indian writer Rabindranath Tagore's conception of nationalism, or rather his rebuttal of it. He wanted a new India in which the English invader would have a place: 'Now at last has come the turn of the English to become true to this history and bring to it the tribute of their life, and we neither have the right nor the power to exclude this people from the building of the destiny of India.' But he did not want an Indian nation that would have a coherent sense of national mission. He wanted an Indian society that would continue with its historic effort to bring cultures and traditions together. Indian independence, as he desired it, would not be about driving the British out and running the country without them, but about assimilating them as India had assimilated previous invaders.

Tagore would not have understood modern Irish nationalism. He would have approved the effort to create a society in which diversity was accommodated, indeed valued as enriching, but he might have had difficulty grasping why this had to be done within the boundaries of a single jurisdiction. He would have urged us to get on with the job of getting to know and love each other and would have seen no reason to create a nation state within which to do that. In fact, the work of creating a nation would only get in the way of bringing people together.

He saw the nation as 'mechanical', an organisation of human purpose which diminished the humanity of the people governed by it. The nation was 'the organised self-interest of a whole people, where it is least human and least spiritual'. His example, of course, was Britain, which had taken control of India. The answer to that problem was not for India to become a coherent sovereign nation, but for it to be a society.

Of course, the British didn't stay in India. You see very few white faces on a Delhi street, though you do often see people with a touch of red in their hair, indicative perhaps of British (or Irish) forebears.

But Tagore's ideas, applied to Ireland, would have prioritised the assimilation of the Anglo-Irish and the northern Protestants into a larger culture enriched by them. Hoping to create an Irish state which those people would ultimately and just grudgingly come to terms with was getting things the wrong way round. Nationalism, he said, was 'a cruel epidemic of evil that is sweeping over the human world of the present age, and eating into its moral vitality' (Tagore, 2010).

Tagore was writing at a time when he could talk of the parts of the world that had not yet formed into nations and saw much of Asia like that. However, Ireland doesn't have the option of not being a nation. The country is not trying to organise itself into a nation for the purpose of conquering other nations and building an empire. It is seeking only to be a trading nation at peace with its separate elements and fit to feed its population so that the young don't have to emigrate.

The purpose of Irish nationalism is only to make Ireland distinct from Britain. It has no other shared purpose, mechanical or otherwise.

George Orwell used the term nationalism to describe political ideologies about which adherents were obsessed and unreasoning. Irish republicanism was a form of nationalism, as was Trotskyism. Like Dunt, Orwell listed the attributes of nationalism. It was, he said, obsessive, unstable and indifferent to reality. He wrote that every form of nationalism was blind to simple truths that contradicted it. His example of Ireland's blindness was the fact that the country depended on the protection of Britain. He was writing at the time of the Second World War.

Fintan O'Toole made basically the same point in an article mocking the state of the Irish Defence Forces in a week in which

Russia had been persuaded not to conduct military exercises close to the Irish fishing fleet. He wrote: 'It would be vastly too expensive to create and maintain a real air force. Better to admit that the RAF does that job.' (*The Irish Times*, 3 Feb. 2022.)

But does the current aspiration for a united Ireland fit with these definitions of nationalism?

Orwell (1945) described Celtic nationalism, Scottish, Irish and Welsh, as 'a belief in the past and future greatness of the Celtic peoples'. He saw in it 'a strong tinge of racialism'. He said, 'The Celt is supposed to be spiritually superior to the Saxon – simpler, more creative, less vulgar, less snobbish etc.' This is the self-image of the Irish we noted above that Daniel O'Connell enthused about.

But are Irish nationalists racist? Not as much as back in 1945 when Orwell was writing this, nor are they perhaps just as possessed of that sense of being spiritually superior. And people like Neale Richmond and Matthew O'Toole do not appear to be obsessive and unreasoning in their aspiration to see Ireland united. They make a case for Irish unity that does not draw on the past. They are not trying to carry forward the project of the Fenian movement, as were Patrick Pearse and Gerry Adams. They present an argument mainly that Ireland as a single economy inside the European Union would be more prosperous.

Sinn Féin is in the Fenian tradition. The Provisional movement traces its mission back to the Easter Rising. But the republican aspiration has changed many times, from seeking a Catholic Ireland to seeking socialist revolution; from rejecting the legitimacy of the Dáil to entering it; from opposing capitalism, to inviting and facilitating capital investment from abroad;

from opposing EU membership to endorsing it, though only apparently because it might provide an added motivation for the one unchanging principle that drives them: creating a single island jurisdiction and writing the IRA into the story as a creative and helpful, noble and self-sacrificing guide along the way.

Some would argue that people like Richmond are indifferent to reality in that they apparently fail to grasp how adamantly unionists reject the unification of Ireland, but a similar charge could be levelled at Doug Beattie and other unionists, that they simply refuse to see the obvious drift towards unity in demographic change and the shock of Brexit. For Brexit not only took northerners out of the EU against their will, it also demonstrated that the Union was not in any meaningful sense a partnership, but rather a relationship in which the senior partner makes the crucial decisions.

10

UP FROM THE COUNTRY

SOMETIMES I WONDER if the Irish Republic itself is a coherent nation, there is such rivalry between counties and provinces.

Gaelic sports differ from British football in a particular way. In Britain, teams represent cities, in Ireland they represent counties, suggesting that in Ireland the roots of sport are more rural than urban. And in Ireland a county team is selected from people who live in that county, while players for Liverpool or Sunderland may have grown up in any part of the country or outside it and may be bought and sold between teams. This Irish way seems to have more integrity to it.

A team representing Tyrone or Kilkenny really does have its roots there and its main support base is also from the home county. The supporters of Manchester United come from all over the world now. In Ireland, thousands of people travel to matches to cheer on a team that has been traditionally supported in their family.

As a big game approaches in Gaelic sport, news programmes visit primary schools in the counties to interview the pupils of a player or the people who knew him as a boy and recognised his promise. Nothing like that happens in English football coverage. We don't get to see the kids in a Manchester school cheering for a player they are personally acquainted with. They are very unlikely to know a player personally because players are professionals on big money and move in a different world.

You also see this Irish regionalism in the annual *Rose of Tralee* festival. When Dáithí Ó Sé is on the stage interviewing the next contestant from Monaghan, he'll turn to the audience and shout, 'Anybody here from Monaghan tonight?' And a corner of the stadium will erupt with the Monaghan people waving flags and banners for their Rose.

People in Ireland like to be flattered according to their county. They still retain a love of the local. Daniel O'Connell appealed to that county identity in his campaign for the repeal of the Union. He was knitting together an Irish Catholic nation, but he was addressing people at county level, urging them to take pride in their neighbours and their surroundings and their local history. In a speech delivered at Mullaghmast in September 1843, he said:

> Oh, there is a starlight sparkling from the eye of a Kildare beauty that is scarcely equalled, and could not be excelled, all over the world. And remember that you are the sons, the fathers, the brothers, and the husbands of such women, and a traitor or a coward could never be connected with any of them … I am in a county where the lamp of Kildare's holy shrine burned with its sacred fire, through ages of darkness and storm.

Not a lot of politicians today speak as floridly as that.

Some commentators have argued that the political life of Ireland operates so much at county level that it has actually hindered the development of a sense of national responsibility. This was the case made by sociologist J.P. O'Carroll in his paper 'Strokes, Cute Hoors and Sneaking Regarders: The Influence of Local Culture on Irish Political Style'. He argued that local culture in Ireland portrayed society as bad and community as good. The county, even the parish, would always be wary of the state and promote its own values as of primary concern when the two clashed.

O'Carroll claimed that community in Ireland was ideological 'in three senses of the word'. It expressed an ethos. That ethos was used to control others, and the emotions roused often got in the way of pursuing the public interest. He also argued that many of the themes developed at community level resonated with nationalism.

What strikes me about this analysis is that it could be applied to republican communities in Northern Ireland where that same dynamic applies. The community is presented as the touchstone of what is right, people are expected to show loyalty to the community – 'don't forget where you come from' – and the interest represented by the community is stronger and often antithetical to the wider interest of society as a whole.

There is a long tradition in Ireland of local forces establishing and enforcing laws of their own making. This stems from the Whiteboys of the eighteenth century and goes right up to the IRA in modern times. In the 1970s I often heard the IRA referred to as 'the boys', suggesting a lineage in custom. A remnant in slang perhaps is the expression 'boyo'. 'He's a boyo' means he makes his own rules. I suspect not all cultures have such affectionate terms for rogues.

In Northern Ireland this thinking legitimised an actual

disregard for the law, and even sabotage and murder. You don't have to look deeply into the roots of violence there to see that what stung people was more the affront to the locality, the community, than the insult to the nation. It was the armed British soldier on the street that offended, less so the politician uttering humbug on the TV screen.

This is not to suggest that love of the county team in Kilkenny or Waterford can escalate into violence. In fact, it is the English football system, without its authentic connection to community, that has generated the greater violence among football supporters.

A good example of a 'boyo' in today's politics is Michael Healy-Rae. An independent TD from Kerry, he flouts the metropolitan norms, for instance by refusing to switch off his mobile phone in the Dáil chamber to signal that he has more important things to deal with than the debate going on in front of him. Healy-Rae illustrated the tension between a national or global interest and a local one when he criticised the then Taoiseach for saying that he would cut down on his consumption of meat in recognition of the damage cattle farming was doing to the environment:

> We have a Taoiseach [Leo Varadkar] that thought it was a good idea to come out and say that he was going to reduce his carbon footprint by reducing the amount of meat he was going to eat, like he forgot he was the Taoiseach for the whole of the country. He's not a Taoiseach for Dublin. And we are predominantly a farming nation, you know. He was turning his backside to all the farmers in Ireland. (joe.ie, 5 March 2019.)

Healy-Rae makes the point that to be a national politician you have to be elected locally. O'Carroll's critique of the way in which local interests constrain national politics perhaps doesn't take that simple point under serious consideration. He was writing about an Ireland in which Fianna Fáil thrived by catering for local concerns, but the first Healy-Rae of the Kerry political dynasty broke away from Fianna Fáil.

Jackie Healy-Rae had been an energetic organiser at local level for the party but turned his skills against his comrades when they declined to select him as a candidate. Two of his sons, Michael and Danny, are now independent TDs and Michael has said that his own son has ambitions for a political career. Their approach is entirely based on fostering their own popularity within their constituencies and they have been mocked in Dáil debates for it.

Michael has brought busloads of Kerry people to Belfast for cataract surgery under a cross-border scheme that enables them to get treatment faster than they could at home. An advertisement lays out a timetable of twenty-minute clinics at a list of Kerry pubs, though it's hard to imagine how he could keep to schedule. But there appears to be no ideology. The family is in politics to get votes and use influence in their constituencies to get more votes and more influence.

Michael Healy-Rae has argued for learner drivers to be allowed to drive unaccompanied. His brother Danny, who runs a pub named after their father, wanted the law changed to give country people permits allowing them to drink up to two pints of beer and drive home. They are eccentrics.

That sense of county differences was picked up by a northern Protestant living in Dublin. Davy Adams, when working with the charity Goal, discovered that Kerry people are 'the nicest people in Ireland'. He says:

> I must have worked with ten or twelve people from Kerry over the years and without exception they were brilliant people and I always said, when a new one came in, I suppose you know I'm resolved never to visit Kerry because knowing my luck I'd meet the only fucker in the county. Obviously you can't generalise like that, but I never met anyone from Kerry that wasn't a fantastic person.

He thinks that the close identification of people by locality is a particularly southern thing and that northerners don't do it: 'It doesn't replicate in the North among the Protestant community. No one cares whether you are from County Down or County Antrim unless you have a strange accent and that's why they are asking. But this competitiveness in Ireland comes from being separated into parishes and being loyal to your own parish, and the competitiveness of GAA as well.'

I don't agree. There are strong local identities in parts of the North. Derry is often spoken of as having native characteristics. The Derry stereotypes are that they are all great singers and that they are so closely attached to family that they can never stay away for long. A friend of mine once joked: 'How come Newry doesn't think it's the centre of the universe?' His point being that Newry is the same size as Derry and similarly located on one end of the border where it meets the sea.

People in west Belfast profess a pride in community expressed through the West Belfast Festival, or Féile, combined with a sense of having experienced the violence of the Troubles more intimately than other areas. And this has been cultivated along the lines that O'Carroll identified, to reinforce a political ideology, in this case the Provisional republicanism of Sinn Féin.

I have also heard people talk of 'a real Shankill character', as if people raised on the Shankill Road in Belfast had an authenticity and a native understanding of Ulster loyalism that could not be acquired from study by someone living in Fortwilliam or Andersonstown. The two markers of difference, disqualifying someone from all hope of empathy with the local, are class and religion, the stronger of these being class.

So, when we ask if Ireland can be one, are we faced with a bigger challenge than just bringing Northern Ireland under the governance of Dáil Éireann?

11

UNIONISM

I HAD A Protestant girlfriend who believed in a united Ireland. I met her one early summer evening on the Ormeau Road in Belfast. This was before the big Orange parades were barred from the lower end of the road where the population was mostly Catholic. The bands would thunder their drums and the whole tone of the parade would tend to get louder and more aggressive when passing there.

There was one such parade that evening. We had heard it approach from the south, a police vehicle leading the way the first we saw of it. I was wary near these parades but not enough to get away from them when they were passing. You have to remind yourself sometimes that the drummers and the baton twirlers are scowling at the whole world, not just at you in particular.

'It just makes more sense,' said Kate. 'They would have far more influence in an all-Ireland parliament than they have here.'

I'd heard this argument before but thought it wasn't gentle reasoning that was going to placate the thundering rage now within a few feet of us.

I said, 'Will you tell them or will I?'

The power of their numbers and the noise they made was their irrefutable case.

But was there more to it.

This was before Brexit made a united Ireland attractive to people who had not dwelt much on the idea before. It was in the early stages of the Peace Process when more than twenty-five years of an IRA campaign had proven futile against the hard reality of demographics and voting patterns. Their position was assured. The Union was in no danger. But still they beat their drums like they were beating the heads of their enemies.

The unionist people are uniformly Protestant and most are presbyterian. They are the descendants of Scots settlers given land here in the seventeenth century after the collapse of the old Gaelic order. Hundreds of years have passed since then and that population has been diluted and fragmented, but it has defined itself by religion and maintained distinctions framed by the wars that followed the Reformation, wars that are long over as far as the rest of Britain is concerned.

Professor Pól Ó Dochartaigh, speaking at the Ireland's Future meeting in Galway, remarked on how surnames inherited from that time may link a person back to that Planter stock but not necessarily, so much having changed since then. Many famous nationalist and republican names came over with the plantation. McDonald, Hume, Adams and Anderson are Scottish names. Sands is an Anglo-Saxon name from Surrey. Hughes is Welsh. Arlene Foster's maiden name is Kelly, but, although this name is generally considered to have Irish origins, she may be one of the Kellys of the Scottish borders. The Protestant-identifying unionists of Northern Ireland are largely of Scottish lineage.

Over the centuries, there has been intermarriage and

religious conversion. In both the nationalist Catholic and unionist Protestant traditions there are old insults for those who cross over. The Catholic who breaks from tradition may be called a souper, one who changed religion to take soup from evangelical preachers. The Protestant defector from the cause of unionism may be called a Lundy, in reference to Robert Lundy, the Governor of Londonderry reviled as a traitor for suggesting capitulation to James II and whose effigy is still burned every year in Derry.

Former UDA man Davy Adams, who worked in Dún Laoghaire, says:

> People used to say to me occasionally, 'You Church of Ireland, Davy? My granny was Church of Ireland or my da was Church of Ireland.' And I would say to myself – up north that's thought of as being a turncoat. And the craturs were trying to find a commonality with you, and I was thinking to myself, if, you're ever up north don't be boasting on either side that you've changed your religion.

There are other insults for Catholics. A 'Castle Catholic' was one who served the British administration. A 'token taig' was a Catholic who sat among unionists to take the bad look off their sectarian character. More secular unionists like Doug Beattie have tried to uncouple this ideology from tradition and impress people who are not Protestants with the good sense of remaining in the UK for the good of all.

Unionism was an ideology that was cultivated by Britain in Ireland, the conviction that Britain and Ireland should be joined together in one kingdom. This was done through the Act of Union of 1800. A new century and a new beginning to pacify Ireland after revolution. But Ireland was never going to be at ease in the UK and by 1922 the country was partitioned, with the two parts separated in different degrees from Great Britain. The detachment of Northern Ireland from the rest of the island through devolution was satisfactory to unionists. They had campaigned against Home Rule for the whole island, but they accepted it for six counties because they would be in charge. Some unionists later campaigned for full reintegration, though this was never a popular position. Ian Paisley senior took this view for a time after the introduction of direct rule in 1972. Most unionists, however, campaigned for the restoration of their devolved government in Stormont and this was so important to them that they were ultimately willing to share power with republicans in a devolved government rather than continue with direct rule or press on for integration.

Even now, when they fear that they are being nudged out of the Union by a border down the Irish Sea, none yet argue that the best reassurance would be reintegration into Britain. So, for all that they insist they are fully British, they prefer to be at a remove. This has shown up often in their social legislation too, where they have preferred more conservative laws on homosexuality and abortion than those enacted in Britain.

Nearly all unionists see direct rule as undesirable, even those who oppose the Good Friday Agreement. They accept, therefore, that their position is bound up with that of the northern nationalists and that there is no prospect of separation from them. So they are British, but not on the same basis as, say, Yorkshire or Cornwall.

Their British nationalism is different from Irish nationalism which, in its pure form, seeks the integration of Northern Ireland and the Republic into a single unit, governed centrally. There is no united Britain vision comparable to the united Ireland vision of nationalists. Some nationalists foresee a united Ireland in which power and some degree of autonomy are devolved to Stormont, but no one seems passionate about the idea.

If a Stormont parliament devolved from Dublin was structured in the same way as the current Stormont, with essential power-sharing, Sinn Féin would be able to abort it by walking out, thereby forcing Dublin to take full control. There have been many such threats to the stability of Stormont already, so it may finally be restructured in such a way that walking out would not bring it down. If such a model could be found, then devolution from Dublin might work.

If nationalist commitment to a united Ireland was identical in character to the unionist commitment to Britain, they would accept devolution from Dublin. Unionists like a semi-detached relationship. Maybe, after a time, nationalists and republicans would find that they would prefer that too.

So what is this Britishness, if unionists want to be governed from London but make decisions for themselves? They say the National Health Service is an important part of it, yet they have let it fall into disrepair. The welfare state may be the incentive for nationalists to retain the Union, yet unionists opposed it at its formation. Even a senior Catholic civil servant in Stormont, Patrick Shea, feared that the Northern Ireland parliament would be reduced to a mere agent of Britain if it had to follow British guidelines on welfare expenditure (Shea, 1981).

The monarchy is also important to unionists, but the monarch is not actually the ruler of the country in any meaningful way. The office connects the present to the historic past but the reigning monarch is essentially a figurehead. Still, it is hard for those of us who are cynical about the monarchy to enter into the thinking of those who are devoted to it and we cannot deny that that devotion is real. Indeed, the streets of Dublin and Cork fall silent for British Royal weddings, suggesting that you do not even have to be a subject to feel reverence for the one whose head bears the crown. All this is utterly bewildering as far as I am concerned. Yet some former British colonies, such as Canada and Australia, despite being fully independent in practice, still enjoy the cosy fiction that the British monarch is their head of state.

If I was in the British government and seeking to assuage unionist fears, I would urge that some young royal be crowned prince or princess of Northern Ireland. There is, after all, a Prince of Wales, so why not? The title would be a bit cumbersome, but a Prince of Ulster would appall the Irish when three counties of Ulster are part of the Republic. The title Prince of Scotland has merged with that of Great Steward of Scotland and is traditionally held by the eldest son of the reigning monarch. There has been a Duke of Edinburgh, so why not a Duke of Belfast?

Unionism is less emphatically Protestant than it used to be. Rev. Ian Paisley included many Anglicans within the sweep of his wrath as an ardent opponent of ecumenism, the effort of Christian Churches to draw closer together. Mainstream unionism rallied behind him, both as their MEP with the highest vote and then as First Minister, but they perhaps indulged him in some of his eccentricities rather than fell ardently into line.

I once travelled with Paisley in a campaign car when he was urging people to come out in a local council area referendum to vote against an ice rink being opened on a Sunday. I could tell that many who flocked around him to enjoy his charm had no intention of actually voting to deny skaters their weekend excitement.

The Protestant character of unionism creates the impression that most if not all of those who want the Union also want gays denied the right to marry and would prefer that women who want abortions should have them in England, Ulster presumably being holier ground. Social attitude surveys routinely show up Protestants as being more socially conservative, but I sometimes wonder if people claim principles that don't mean much to them for the sake of appearing to be different from those they oppose.

One of the stereotypes preserved in Northern Ireland is that Protestants are more industrious and Catholics more verbose and gregarious. The reasoning follows from the idea that Protestants put less value on education because their attitudes were formed in the heavy industries where jobs were reserved for them, while Catholics had to pass exams to become teachers and priests and solicitors. This has become a cliché, yet it presumes that young Protestants today have attitudes framed in heavy industries that died out forty years ago. Where you do find big engineering plants now is in Tyrone, which is predominantly Catholic.

There might be some truth in these perceptions. Unionists are, by this stereotype, seen to be suspicious of tricky language and like things to be stated plainly. I gathered a sense of that when providing media skills workshops to loyalist groups in Belfast, but probably their fear of deft argument is widespread among those who have less experience of debate, whatever community they belong to.

The unionists' sense of community as distinct from the rest of Ireland was maintained through congregations and political parties. More recently, perhaps as secularisation erodes congregations, some have sought to revive and reinforce an Ulster Scots identity and language. Nationalists similarly might be getting more fervent about the Irish language as a definer now that Catholicism is on the wane.

Ulster unionism also congregates around the memorialisation of war, as most communities do, and the wars that matter most to them are the Battle of the Boyne when the Dutch Protestant William defeated the Catholic King James II, and the First World War, particularly the Battle of the Somme where the 36th Ulster Division suffered massive losses. Nationalists and unionists both argued that their people should fight for Britain in that war, and that Britain would repay the debt. Unionism cherished that memory, while nationalism set it aside for decades, preferring to forget that far more of their own people had died in the trenches than ever fought for Irish freedom.

In recent years it has been possible to think of the memorialisation of the Great War as unifying traditions in Ireland in joint sorrow for unthinkable losses. Doug Beattie is trying to remind people today of similar shared experience between

Irish and British soldiers who fought together in Afghanistan and Iraq.

*

The Ulster Protestant people represent a mixing of two nations and are no more British than they are Irish. They are a distinct people. Obviously they are not all alike. Some, like my friend Kate, actually want a united Ireland. Others, like Wallace Thompson, define their Britishness by the monarchy alone and would consider being part of a new Ireland if the monarchy ceased to be Protestant. There are class divisions among Protestants and some have secularised, so we are not talking about an homogenous people, but in reality no people is homogenous.

Many unionists are happy to describe themselves as Irish. Few would say that they aren't Irish at all, even as they insist on the Union with Britain. The parents of Mervyn Gibson, the general secretary of the Orange Order, lived in Donegal. Willie Haye was born in Donegal and is now a DUP member of the House of Lords. He refuses to pay for British citizenship because he feels he should be naturally entitled to it. Both men say they are primarily British and are determined to remain British.

But Great Britain is the name of the island of England, Scotland and Wales. The designation when Northern Ireland is included is the United Kingdom of Great Britain and Northern Ireland. So it is nominally dubious to describe Northern Ireland as British.

The Irish nationalist says that the unionist is a deluded Irish person who will accept an Irish identity when the Union has gone. Some evidence of this is that British-identifying Protestants who stayed on in the Irish Free State, later the Republic, assimilated well. Neale Richmond believes that the acceptance of his forebears that they are Irish suggests that northern Protestants will settle down as easily.

Some might say that those southern Protestants had no choice, since their numbers were small, and intermarriage and secularisation eroded their communities and congregations, but that a million northern unionists would be harder to swallow. Might the vehemence of unionists in declaring their Britishness betray a doubt?

Loyalist violence was vicious. Why did so many of them direct their energies against people who were no threat to them or to the Union? Of course, they had every right to be angry about terrorism, but why did so many not just leave it to the state to suppress the IRA? Of course, most unionists did. Why did they not trust in the obvious fact that the IRA had no prospect of forcing a united Ireland?

Once I was on a platform at a debate in Hillsborough organised by the Orange Order. Mervyn Gibson made a speech about how the Orange movement had defended the Union. I said I thought that was daft because the survival of the Union was never in doubt.

So why did unionists and loyalists doubt that the Union would survive? They seemed to be taking the IRA on its own evaluation of itself as an army at war engaged in a viable effort to claim Northern Ireland for the Republic. Yet it never had the remotest prospect of achieving that.

But if they really thought the Union was under threat, how did political unionism rally massive crowds in denial of the

Anglo-Irish agreement, then cave in so lightly. Where had all the ardour gone? Have unionists, like the Protestants in the South, learned more easily than expected to adapt to what they had previously abhorred?

Unionism has seemed coherent and colossal in crisis, but in quieter times more diffuse.

12

UNIONISTS IN A UNITED IRELAND

CONSIDER HOW BRITISH-IDENTIFYING Ulster Protestants might react if they are voted into a united Ireland. We might assume that most would accept the dissolution of the Union and their citizenship within a new state, albeit one against which they virtually defined themselves for over a century. They will not have the same fear they had in previous generations that Ireland would be dominated by the Catholic Church. Nor would they fear that a predominantly agricultural Ireland would be an uneasy fit with the industrial North. These were authentic concerns that they saw as warranting partition in the past. They are not now.

Ireland has good roads and infrastructure. The heavy industries around Belfast are gone, so both parts of the island might cooperate to develop a modern economy without fearing that the other would drag it down. The greater fear might be on the part of the South, which does not have the same dependency on state subventions and a massive public service.

So let's imagine the new Ireland and the Ulster Protestants within it.

Neale Richmond and others will have campaigned for a recognition of British citizenship within the new republic to minimise any sense of grievance. The unionists will not be unionists any more, but they will have their flag, their culture, British passports and even, perhaps, British driving licences, he says. All this is being allowed for in some of the current efforts to imagine a new state.

And once the vote has been carried for a united Ireland it is inconceivable that any route might open through which it could be reversed. Britain will have accepted that Northern Ireland is not in the Union. It will not be amenable to taking those six counties back if things don't work out happily. That will be Ireland's responsibility.

So what might unhappy unionists do?

Neale Richmond, Hubert Butler and others have been quoted in earlier chapters describing how the Protestants in the Republic settled into defining themselves confidently as Irish and retaining such culture as was contained within school traditions, sport, churches and community. This gives hope that Protestants in a new Ireland would settle down and be happily Irish.

In the past, assimilation in the South was no doubt hindered by sectarian discrimination and the special position of the Catholic Church. However, there is little reason to worry about those factors now, so perhaps we can expect that assimilation might be faster. But let's imagine how difficult those disgruntled, ill-at-ease British-identifying Protestants might make things.

The Protestants in the North are not going to spread out throughout the island and get dissolved into the larger social context. They are concentrated in specific territories. Chiefly they occupy two counties in the northeast: Antrim and Down. They also have communities in several other towns and cities, and within these towns and cities they live in definably distinct areas.

The border will have gone, but there will remain a much more complicated dividing line between Catholic and Protestant communities in places like Belfast, Derry, Ballymena, Newry and Armagh; indeed, practically everywhere across the North. We know from experience that northern communities which predominate in territorial areas like housing estates, villages, towns or parts of towns tend to impose their identity on their physical surroundings. They do this with murals that declare their allegiance or celebrate their heroes, with flags and bunting, graffiti and painted kerbstones. It seems likely that Protestant and specifically loyalist communities will maintain and amplify that tradition in order to distance themselves from the new Ireland.

Along with territorial declarations like this comes trouble at interfaces, particularly at times like the Twelfth or the night before it. Currently 'peace lines' separate these communities and there is no outcry to remove those dividing walls, despite the clamour for the removal of the Irish border. We are talking about uniting Ireland while it still remains impossible to unite these communities. This might be getting things the wrong way round.

The problem with territory that gets defined as sectarian and exclusive is that people leave who do not feel comfortable in the marked surroundings, and the factional character becomes even more concentrated. In such areas, property values decline, industry stays away and unemployment and social deprivation increase. With these changes the sense of grievance deepens.

Although this Protestant homeland, as we might call it, will not be a single coherent unit at first, it could develop into one around a large consolidation of Protestant population in Antrim and Down. If tensions turned violent, as in the past, the likely strategic aim of violent loyalist forces would be to remove Catholics from parts of that territory to enable a clearer boundary to be drawn. It hardly seems conceivable that such a territory or homeland could realistically aspire to independence or to reunification with Britain or with an independent Scotland, but it could represent a perpetually tangible and conspicuous factory of grievance; an Irish Gaza perhaps with a population of half a million people and high unemployment among them.

We can't expect that violence would stop because the issue of the constitution had been settled.

The Protestants of the South settled in after partition because they were a wealthier class with a stake in the country's survival and because they were largely rural and spread out and therefore unlikely to consolidate territorially. They may also have felt a need to disassociate themselves from the Protestants in the North, who were governing through discrimination and expressing their culture through triumphalist Orangeism.

An Orange enclave in the new Ireland would be wholly different in character to the communities of Protestants which remained in the South after partition. It might not feel the same incentives to present itself as docile and obliging.

Also, it might be simplistic to assume that the constitution is all that people were fighting over, just because they said so.

What did wild Protestant and Catholic teenagers know of the constitution when they first took to the streets? We might find out that that is not what the problem was at all, that sectarianism was real and fundamental, and that the hate and fear that simmers at certain times of the year had not gone away, had not been settled by a referendum because the question had been the wrong question after all. There was violent sectarianism before partition and even before the Union.

Because they will mark out territory, the Protestants who wish to protest will be able to do so together in places that they are familiar with and in council areas in which they already have a political presence. They will be able to put the stamp of their British identity on those places and establish social structures, institutions and routines for the preservation of that identity. From those territories they will be able to express their dissatisfaction or even contempt for the Irish state.

Whatever grievances they have, they will be able to organise around and assert. They will control local government and send members to the national parliament. Those members will have the potential to be a much bigger headache than the Healy-Raes.

In their local government areas and segregated housing estates they will already have institutions and social structures through which to represent their dissatisfaction. They will have the churches, the loyal orders, political parties and paramilitary organisations. The current estimate of membership of one paramilitary organisation, the Ulster Defence Association, is 6,000.

Protestant unionist identity tends to become more emphatic when it is challenged. We can anticipate that many Protestant communities will settle down quite easily, much preferring stable conditions for business. But others will be truculent.

The estimate usually cited is that Northern Ireland has a million Protestants. This assessment can be dismissed as meaningless in that many of those included within the number are not Protestant in any meaningful sense. Many have close family relationships with Catholics through intermarriage. And many have already decided that peace is more important than division. Many recognise that they are Irish. They want the Union but recognise that a day may come when they can't have what they want.

How then might we estimate the scale of resistance that will emerge? Perhaps we can calculate it from the electoral bases of the most ardent unionist politicians, but that figure would include many who are not just as ardent themselves, who may be voting tactically, either to keep out a nationalist candidate or, pragmatically, to return a favour. Who knows? The vote itself on the border poll would give us some idea, but even that might exaggerate the number that would be downright stroppy in their refusal to be compliant citizens.

Let's assume that half a million Protestants might fit that category. That would represent about a tenth of the Irish population. These people have tradition, they have origins in the Plantation and they have religion in common. Suppose they choose to identify themselves as an ethnic minority vulnerable to oppression. If they did so, they would be larger than any other ethnic group, whether the travellers or migrants. As a protest movement they would be larger perhaps than organisations which campaign for sexual orientation and gender rights. And then we might ask what they would demand if they organised themselves, which, as we have established, they could easily do.

They would first of all demand recognition as a distinct ethnic group entitled to special consideration. They would want equality monitoring to ensure that they were not discriminated against in employment or disbursal of public funds. That's fair enough. That already exists in Northern Ireland, where such legislation was introduced to protect a Catholic minority and then extended to other groups.

They would fly the Union Jack or Ulster flag from all public buildings in their territories.

They would ask for reserved places in public employment, like the civil service and the police. There are examples of this elsewhere in the world, like the Indian legislation protecting scheduled castes. Indeed, the Police Service of Northern Ireland was set up on the principle that Catholics should have guaranteed places. They might demand that 10 per cent of the Garda Síochána be Protestant, or alternatively that the PSNI be retained as a separate constabulary in the North with 50 per cent Protestant representation.

They might insist on Ulster Scots street names in Protestant areas. They could use their collective pull as an underprivileged ethnic group to demand funding for festivals and monuments to mark Ulster British heroes. They might change street names and the names of railway stations and bridges to celebrate Carson, Craig, Paisley and the British monarch.

They may demand public holidays for their special occasions like the Twelfth and the monarch's birthday. They will surely resist any ruling that Irish language be a compulsory subject in their secondary schools.

They will campaign, undoubtedly, for Ireland to rejoin the Commonwealth. They will be able to argue that Ireland is exceptional among former colonies in refusing.

They will use their status as a minority ethnic group to demand special consideration. That will be leverage around other issues that we cannot predict.

And where demands are resisted they may grow. If the state used violence against protests, resistance would deepen and grievance would spread to neighbours who were not initially committed.

*

Of course, there is another northern ethnic group: the nationalists. In the view of Cork comedian Tadhg Hickey, these are simply Irish people who have been dumped and deserted but whose community has evolved over the hundred years since partition. It has lived within a wholly different political and media culture to that of people in the South. They – we – are different, but what happens to that difference after unification? The key aspiration of northern nationalist political parties will have been met. Will this community still have a purpose? Will it suffer from a loss of purpose? Will it come under a stronger presumption that it should simply dissolve into the Irish nation and find that declarations of distinction will not be indulged? Is it likely to be patronised a little when it engages in the big debates, told that it can't really be expected to fully understand?

Noticeably Sinn Féin, as the advance guard of northern politics into the South, has tended not to field northerners for seats in the Dáil. Even they seem to accept that the northern nationalist is different and might not be as fully at home in the South as the theory of nationalism presumes.

Much of the political caché of the northern nationalists derives from a fear that if they are confronted, they may turn violent, or, to put it more softly and diplomatically, that community sensitivities need to be handled with care. So, for instance, you get a massive IRA funeral in Belfast with the police keeping their distance, having been advised to do so by a former IRA prisoner on the policing board. Would that community continue to claim the right to be handled with care in a united Ireland? In the North, at present, the umbrage against such indulgence comes mainly from unionists who get indulged themselves in other circumstances, like the police looking the other way while they build massive dangerous bonfires.

In the new Ireland the section of society likely to sneer at these accommodations of militarised communal assertions will basically be everybody else, now four-fifths of the country. The special pleading that allows communities to stretch the law and plead favour, not just in policing but in government funding, is likely to be less effective when the North is part of the larger polity.

A recurring complaint of unionists in northern author Sam McAughtry's book *Down in the Free State* is that the Irish in Northern Ireland withdrew from the state and denied it a chance to find coherence and stability. Unionists might well do the same in the new Ireland. The state may want to include and embrace a tetchy minority, but it may not be given the chance.

Dan Hannan, a former Conservative MEP, argued in the *Washington Examiner* of 20 December 2021 that Britain allows

Irish people to be British in a way that Ireland does not allow British people to be Irish. He wrote:

> Northern Ireland cannot be incorporated into either of its neighbouring states without disappointing a big chunk of its population. The British government has always recognized that challenge. Hence its support for power-sharing, its readiness to let people in Northern Ireland take Irish passports and proclaim Irish nationality, and its willingness to let Irish nationals within Great Britain vote, claim social security, and exercise other rights as full citizens. Because so many British (including this author) have Irish family links, Ireland will never be seen simply as a foreign state in the way that, say, Finland is.
>
> Oddly, though, the reverse does not apply. Every time Ireland has had to choose, it has emphasized its distance from Britain rather than trying to appeal to Northern Unionists.

Neale Richmond tweeted a comment on this, describing the article as toxic, which sparked a debate, with many unionists agreeing with the article and even some declared nationalists saying that though they didn't agree with it they could respect it as a point of view. Perhaps the fact that so many Protestants in the South adapted to Irish identity and so many northern Catholics seem content with the Union suggests that these identities are more fluid than they appear to be at times of stress and conflict.

I knew Sam McAughtry in the 1980s. We were both contributors to two separate BBC programmes. I had been brought onto a lunchtime magazine programme called *Talkback* to alternate with Sam in a talk slot. Initially this slot was to feature a day in the life of some character, but it soon morphed into a general opinion piece and, this being during the Troubles, the opinions settled down to routine commentary on the political violence. Sam was a Protestant and I was a Catholic – by background anyway – and that satisfied the BBC's requirement for balance. We also worked on a Sunday morning religious affairs programme called *Sunday Sequence*. Sam contributed talks there too; my work was mostly reportage.

Neither of us were good representatives on *Talkback* of polar extremes of thought. Sam was a Protestant who wanted to know and love the South and who wanted to win his Protestant neighbours over to sympathy with it. In 1996 he was elected to Seanad Éireann. I was no longer a Catholic and I was deeply averse to what I regarded as the simplistic reasoning of stock republicanism. We were so alike in some ways that when Sam got bogged down in writing a book, he asked me to do some of the research for him. I turned him down for I was busy myself. The book emerged as *Down in the Free State*. It was an account of a northern Protestant's journey down the middle of Ireland, from Belfast to Cork, to report back on what little concern people in the South had for the North.

Sam had a theory that both Protestants and Catholics had lost something after partition. The Protestants, he claimed, had been content to think of themselves as Irish until republicanism redefined Irishness as Catholic and Gaelic: 'We sat on a Sunday and listened to the hurling, and we knew all the hurling heroes. We worshipped John McCormack, and when the Pope made him a count of the Holy Roman Empire, we said it was the very least he could have done.'

This all seems overblown sentiment to me and not quite credible, given that Sam was born in the year of partition, 1921, and was only seven years old when John McCormack was honoured by the Pope. I'm having difficulty finding other Protestants who recall their parents or grandparents ever speaking so warmly of the period before division. Yet, Mervyn Gibson and Trevor Ringland and other unionists have little difficulty calling themselves Irish. Mervyn says that he would like to see a united Ireland inside the UK, though he accepts that that is an impossible fantasy. Even so, it expresses affinity with the people of the Republic and not a desire to be wholly separate from them on all terms.

Perhaps Sam spoke for a sense of loss felt after partition when Protestant families in the North might have felt cut off from their cousins in the Free State. Perhaps there was a time when they had to get used to not calling themselves Irish. But Protestants in Tiger's Bay huddled round their radios on a Sunday afternoon listening to the All-Ireland hurling final? I'm not sure I believe that.

The point at which Protestants might legitimately claim that they were betrayed, cut out of a conception of Irishness, would more likely have been the Easter Rising and the War of Independence when Irishmen were killing British soldiers who were regarded by northern Protestants as their own. Pearse and Connolly led the Rising when other Irishmen from throughout the island were fighting and dying in their hordes on the Western Front. Northern Protestants viewed the rebellion as a betrayal and framed the story of their young men lost in battle as part of the founding myth of the new state of Northern Ireland. That is clear still in murals in Protestant parts of Belfast and the honouring of the dead of the Somme. The South wrote its Great War dead out of the foundation story and incorporated instead the much smaller number of dead revolutionaries. That was surely the starkest parting of the ways.

While the Rising and the subsequent executions fired up resistance in most of Ireland and created a readiness for war with Britain, the same event appalled northern Protestants. It was never going to be something with which they could identify, for all the claims on their loyalty in the Proclamation and its guarantees of 'religious and civil liberty'.

Sam's Protestant neighbours had no faith in the South offering a home to Protestants in a united Ireland and harboured a deep sense of having been slighted and scorned – so deep that they preferred not to think of themselves as Irish at all. Sam described the quarrel between North and South as a fight between brothers. He argues in the pub: 'There is no harder fight than a fight between brothers. The bad temper can last for generations, even unto the third and fourth.'

'I'm frigged if I can see what you are on about,' said another man. 'It's simple. The Taigs want a Taig nation.'

So the objection to a united Ireland among some unionists was not to the joining of the two territories into a single nation, but to the type of nation they perceived the Catholic majority to want. It was not a dispute over territory, but over culture and religion.

Sam asked the unionist mayor of Armagh, Sam Foster, if he considered himself Irish. Foster said, 'Well, on St Patrick's Day the RCs are all going to church, but the Protestants are working away just like any other day. Sometimes I think it's a pity, but there you are, that's the way it has to be. They've taken all that side of things over, haven't they?'

There is that same idea that the conflict over Irish unity is a culture war.

I tried out this same idea on my friend George Larmour, a Protestant from the Shankill Road. He said:

> I can't say I recognise Sam McAughtry's perception that Protestants somehow felt some resentment at Catholics hogging the Irish identity to themselves and excluding them.
>
> I'm not sure where he is coming from with that idea.
>
> I can't say that I, or indeed any of my average Protestant family or friends, ever felt that we had any great longing to be classed as Irish, but that we weren't allowed to feel that way because Catholics wouldn't let us or that they stole that aspiration from us – that just doesn't make any sense to me.

In David Ireland's play, *Cyprus Avenue*, Eric Miller, an obsessive loyalist, divulges to his psychiatrist how he allowed himself to be Irish in an Irish pub in London in an evening of drunken elation. He meets another loyalist who tells him a story of a little boy who asked his mummy if they had stolen their land from the Fenians. The play suggests that maintaining a clear, confident unionist identity is challenged all the time by smiling Fenian eyes, the greater confidence of the northern Catholics, the unstated fear that in denying their Irishness, Protestants are denying their true selves.

Perhaps there was a moment in our history when northern Protestants had to painfully reconcile themselves to losing their Irishness, but they no longer hanker for it. 'A Taig nation', as feared by Protestants, would have been a Catholic and Gaelic nation in which they would be culturally excluded from equal citizenship.

In 1974 the UVF in Belfast responded to a proposal by the DUP co-founder Desmond Boal for an 'amalgamated Ireland', a united Ireland with Northern Ireland remaining as an entity with some degree of autonomy, presumably devolved to it from Dublin. The primary concern expressed by loyalists was that Protestants would have complete freedom to express their religion and that the Catholic theocracy in the Republic would come to an end. It sounds bizarre that murderers who bombed Dublin and Monaghan in the same year this statement was made were asserting the right to be Christian in their own way.

UVF leaders met with journalist Vincent Browne and said:

> Our basic objective is to preserve our Protestant liberties and traditions and our British way of life. By that we don't mean the preservation of the link with Britain but of those traditions of religious and civil freedoms which have characterised British democracy. When we talk of the preservation of our Protestant traditions and liberties we simply mean that we want to ensure that we are able to worship God in the manner of our choice and not according to the ordinance or dictate of any outside organisations such as the Catholic church. (*Evening Herald*, 14 Jan. 1974.)

Reading this now it would appear that the loyalist killers of the 1970s should be much more easily reconciled to a united Ireland now that the influence of the Church has declined.

David Porter, an evangelical Christian who is now an adviser to the Archbishop of Canterbury and one of the founders of a group called Evangelical Contribution on Northern Ireland, told me that he had had a moderating insight while on missionary work in Pakistan. He had previously accepted the argument of Ian Paisley and others that Northern Ireland had to remain intact for the preservation of the reformed faith. Then he saw Christian communities in Pakistan which did not need state power on their side to thrive. Why then would Protestants in Northern Ireland need a state or region in which they governed as the majority?

Unionists, at least in the recent past, resented the pressure to enter a united Ireland because they perceived that they were being denied a choice. But they also wanted to remain separate from the rest of Ireland because it was culturally alien to them. And whatever part of the culture wasn't alien had been, as some saw it, appropriated by Catholics and nationalists, so that they couldn't think of it as their own any more.

Pearse's vision contained a contradiction, that Irishness was Gaelic and Catholic and that those who were Protestant and British were deluded about the nature of their real Irish identity. Just how much delusion did they have to shake off to fit with his vision? The Proclamation offered religious liberty, as did the Treaty, but de Valera's Republic privileged the Catholic Church confirming unionist fears that Home Rule would be Rome Rule. They didn't just cut themselves off from the rest of Ireland. Sam McAughtry's interviewees were right; Ireland defined itself in ways that actively excluded them.

Yet while unionism was clinging to a tradition which was external to 'that idea of Irishness', republican conceptions of a united Ireland were actually in constant flux. Today, it is not a Catholic Ireland that they hope to woo them into, but a European, internationalist, liberal and secular Ireland.

13

IRELAND'S FUTURE

IN A LITTLE office in Queen's University sits a placid-natured, soft-spoken, curly-haired academic activist. He is Colin Harvey, a professor of constitutional law and one of the organisers of a group called Ireland's Future (IF), which has been staging debates around the country on how to work towards a united Ireland.

What Colin discovered was that on social media there is little or no space within which to declare a desire for a united Ireland without coming under attack and being accused of being a fanatic. Some have even campaigned for him to be removed from his academic post on the grounds that he is not neutral. He says that, in fact, universities want their academics to be engaged in public debates.

'Like many people here I am both a participant and an observer of conversations. Where people like me can make a contribution is on the preparatory side of all that stuff, thinking through some of the mechanics of the before, during and after. I haven't made any secret of my own preferences and I don't see any contradiction.'

Arguably he comes under so much fire because others who nominally want a united Ireland are doing nothing about it, shrinking from the debate. Colin says:

It has been one of the most baffling things of the last few years that the Irish government has not pushed this. This is a mainstream element of the Good Friday Agreement. It's in the Irish constitution. We're not talking about a marginal discussion. So the Irish government should be front and centre of all the things that people have proposed, a dedicated minister. I like the idea of an all-island citizens' assembly, have people discussing what they would like to see. If you have got an anticipated future, if you've got a region whose constitution says this is based on consent and only consent, it seems to be foolish not to plan – it's almost like a risk assessment, a managerial task.

He is aware of several other academic projects for exploring Irish unity but feels that the debate is inhibited by 'a punch in the face'. In other words, people know that unionists get rattled at the mention of Irish unity and the debate is dampened if not always by fear, then by a desire not to annoy.

'The other aspect of this, oddly absent from the debate, is that we have a way back to the EU. I would like, in my lifetime, to have a vote about returning to the European Union.' Which is not what nationalists usually say they want. Much of European nationalism is facing in the other direction, dreaming of getting out of the EU. Colin says:

We are talking about returning to what is the antithesis of a nationalist vision, a pan-European super-national entity. That unsettles some of the narrative here as well. In a sort of political theory-type nationalist lens, how can it be possible to be making a case for returning to the EU,

which a number of nationalist forces are trying to chip
away at and undermine?

One of the early IF discussions was held in September 2021
in Cork and I thought it was illuminating. The chairperson,
Senator Frances Black, introduced the panel as reflective of
the diversity of the people in Ireland. This was an interesting
starting point.

Historically the division in Ireland over unification is
between nationalists and unionists, with each of those bodies
of thought being internally divided: republicans and loyalists
having more condensed views than the wider communities.
While people of a range of sexual orientations or ethnic roots
will obviously be part of the Ireland of the future with, hopefully,
much to say about the framing of the constitution if it changes,
they have not traditionally been part of the historic argument
that IF believes is coming to a resolution in this generation.

There were no gay companies at the GPO in Easter week. No
doubt there were gay and lesbian people at arms, and some may
have harboured a secret hope that the future would endorse
them, but that is not what the leadership was fighting for. The
very essence of the Irish revolution was an effort to produce an
Irish nation which was Catholic, and therefore heterosexual,
and Gaelic, and therefore white.

So it is a radical rejection of the vision of Pearse and de
Valera to include gays, lesbians, migrants and others in the
discussion, but perhaps IF didn't anticipate how that might
clutter their own debate. Do migrants and gays want rid of the
border? Do they have any agreed thinking among themselves
about it? What hope would there be of mobilising them as

coherent political forces arguing for Irish unity? If I were a gay man or a Somali migrant I might ask, what hope do I have of being accepted in this country which can't even manage to find empathy between unionists and republicans, all of them white and Christian and born within a few hundred miles of each other on the same smallish island?

On the panel of that IF meeting was Laura Harman, who was introduced as a Cork LGBT activist who had campaigned for marriage equality. It also included Tadhg Hickey, the writer and comedian, who would report from a recent trip to Northern Ireland; James O'Connor, the youngest Fianna Fáil TD, who would represent his party's enthusiasm for unity as cool but circumspect; and Karen Sethuraman, the only northern Protestant, a Baptist minister who wanted only to spread the love and hadn't a political notion in her head for much of the debate, at least none that she cared to share.

James O'Connor was the first to speak, when he was asked if the government should lead the way to resolving all-island concerns by creating a health service which was free at the point of need, although Frances Black stopped short of actually saying, 'like the British one'.

O'Connor started out on the side of caution. 'We have to accept that this would take many many years of preparation.' He said he worried that our nearest neighbour, Britain had become an unreliable partner, which takes decisions in its own interests that may not be in the interests of Ireland. That neighbour had the power to call a referendum in the North on Irish unity. He conceded, 'We are definitely on a journey of this question being put to the country.' He expressed the hope that if there was to be a border poll before 2030, Ireland would be prepared.

So his take seemed to be that since the question of whether Ireland should be united into one jurisdiction was going to be raised outside the current jurisdiction, Ireland was vulnerable to being taken by surprise and should be ready. He did not give the impression that he was eager for unity himself.

O'Connor was followed by Karen Sethuraman. If this was to be a frank and focused discussion on the prospect of Irish unity, then a more ardent unionist should have been there. Karen Sethuraman had come as a reconciler, not to assert the unionist position but rather to speak for the Christian hope that we might all love one another. Which we should, of course. Absolutely. She explained that unionists want to be part of the UK and said that's okay, but failed to advance any argument to explain how this could be okay with someone who wanted them to be part of a united Ireland. But she said conversations were already happening. 'And when it comes to our precious unionist community, they need to be part of that.'

She said that she was really keen to hear young people's voices on the question of Ireland's future. She said she had asked a cross-community youth programme if she could pitch three questions to the young people taking part.

'I didn't ask the direct question, do you want a united Ireland, because I don't think that's a starting point.'

Well, it would be if you wanted to know their opinions on that question.

It appeared that Karen Sethuraman liked to keep things vague and unfocussed so that dissension wouldn't emerge. Her questions were: How do we make our home a better place to live? What are your dreams for our future together? and, If there was a message to our politicians and our governments, what would it be? The responses she got included the message that we need to start by making friends with each other, we are all just human beings. This was from Aoife or Eva, aged fourteen. Karen Sethuraman suggested, on the evidence of her magnanimity, that Aoife or Eva be made president.

That was the level of her contribution.

'Sometimes that's the simple message that us oldies who have grown up in tribalism need to hear.'

Another of the young people, Tom, said, 'We need to acknowledge difference, including new people, because we all belong.'

Eventually she got to the point of saying that the common ground was that all agreed that a border poll was coming and she said her message to unionists was, 'You have got to build your vision.'

Jeffrey Donaldson, had he been there, might have told her that he had already done so. The unionist vision is of Northern Ireland remaining part of the UK.

Then we heard from Owodunni Ola Mustapha who came to Ireland in 2014 from Nigeria and had taken part in a Migrant Electoral Empowerment Programme. She and her children lived in Mayo in direct provision. Her chief concern was about the perception of asylum seekers as selfish and uneducated. She said:

> Keeping people wallowing behind the walls of direct provision centres because you feel they are problematic or they are just here as a waste of resources, that's where the problem is majoring. And I think the kind of language that politicians throw out there when it's migrants or lone parents or even people who belong to the LGBT

community is just very dangerous rhetoric that we as the younger generation need to start debunking. Right now, if we are looking for a united Ireland or a better Ireland in the future – I have seen a lot of refugee children, asylum seekers' children who spend decades living in direct provision, going out there and doing fabulous things. It's about giving people the opportunity to try and looking beyond them coming here for the money.

Nobody crosses seven rivers and seven seas only to live off handouts. I would want to work for my living. I would want to give back to the Irish who opened doors for me.

But whether Ireland being united into a whole island jurisdiction would help the assimilation of migrants or not was something she had no apparent opinion on.

Tadhg Hickey was the first to speak passionately about the need for a united Ireland. He started out by saying that he liked the idea that the discussion so far had been apolitical, but he was about to change that. He traced his lifelong republican thinking back to seeing a map when he was a child in which the island of Ireland was two different colours and that had just seemed wrong to him. Hickey argued that, for reconciliation, the South has to reach out to northern nationalists and acknowledge that six counties were sacrificed, 'that we pulled up the drawbridge'. He said, 'The least we can do now is say that was wrong and is still wrong.'

He also picked up on the Republic being called Ireland: 'People in the South now say Ireland and mean the twenty-six counties. We're telling them [northerners] they are not Irish.

They can't vote in presidential elections, they can't vote in RTÉ competitions.'

He had been to Northern Ireland just recently and said: 'I was talking to people who all hang tricolours outside their houses and pubs; they all speak Irish better than I do and they are far more knowledgeable of their history. Calling them not Irish is tantamount to making them stateless and that's a trauma that needs to be looked at.'

It actually is not tantamount to making them stateless, but nobody corrected him on that and he moved on. And I do find it annoying but not actually traumatic that the Republic now calls itself Ireland. People living in the North are entitled to British or Irish passports; they enjoy the benefits of the welfare state and the National Health Service, such as they are. If I had been there I might have stood up to explain to Tadhg Hickey that my family, far from being left stranded in Northern Ireland, had moved there from the Republic for the higher standard of living, better welfare benefits and housing. I might have told Karen Sethuraman that love wasn't going to cut it. And to those impressed by her, I'd have explained that she was most certainly not the voice of unionism. But I wasn't there. I followed the debate later online.

Owodunni Ola Mustapha could have told Tadhg Hickey what being stateless is like and it is not fundamentally about not voting in presidential elections in another jurisdiction nor is it about being unable to enter competitions run by TV stations in that other jurisdiction.

Tadhg Hickey bemoaned the fact that the people of the South know so little about the North. 'The first thing we can do is go visit them ...' This presents an image of tourists coming to look at us and ascertain for themselves that we are Irish.

'The question', he said, 'is not how do we take the North on but how do we sell ourselves to the North.'

He said he believed that unity was inevitable: 'It's coming and it's now a little bit up to unionists to show what the Union has to offer, because even just pure demographics tell you it's on the way.' He argued that the Irish government is not doing enough to prepare. He cited Brendan O'Leary's observation that South Korea has had a minister for unification for fifty years. 'However crazy it is up North, it's not that crazy so we need to get going.'

Following him, Laura Harman said that partition had failed because it was 'extremely ill thought out'. She suggested that there needed to be an all-Ireland citizens' assembly to prepare the way for Irish unity and that it should include travellers and Irish-language speakers.

Speakers from the floor were no more alert to the nuances of the Northern Irish experience than the formal speakers on the panel. One woman in the audience said, 'I don't understand the need for a UK identity but I am not going to fight it.' But if she can't understand the need for a UK identity, how can she understand the need for an Irish one?

The question arose of whether the new united Ireland would retain the tricolour as the national flag. In relation to this James O'Connor said: 'The message of the tricolour is something I often think about and obviously the green and the orange and the peace between, the white. And I think it would be a great shame to lose it.' He said he understood that retaining the national anthem would be 'challenging'. Could unionists really be expected to stand for a republican soldier's song?

If we ever did have a united Ireland we have to remember the wording and the translation because of who we [Fianna Fáil] are in the first opening line. We have to ask ourselves as a nationalist community in the Republic of Ireland, what would that mean to the unionists in Northern Ireland and how inclusive would they feel that would be, remaining in place, but above all else I'd love to see us communicate the meaning of the tricolour. Many people in the Republic of Ireland are not aware of its particular meaning.

Unfortunately for those who see the tricolour as symbolising peace between the Green and Orange traditions, the hope of impressing unionists with that meaning has probably already been lost. In Belfast and Derry the flag is understood by Protestants as a marker of territory and a celebration of militant republican culture.

Tadhg Hickey said it is too early for red lines:

I love the flag but it would be remiss to go into a discussion that throws everything out on the table. I think it's at the end of a process. These conversations at the moment should focus on what does a united Ireland look like. Like we haven't really discussed whether it is some sort of a federacy and Stormont prevails or if it's like a unified Ireland and Stormont is gone. What you don't want is for the secretary of state for Northern Ireland to call a referendum and we have no planning done, because then we don't know what we're trying to sell, so that whatever small hope we have of bringing unionists into a really well thought out plan for what Ireland will look like economically, socially, in terms of the constitution, we have no chance if we don't do that planning.

Then came the interesting turn. Amanullah De Sondy is head of religion at Cork University and he has since taken Irish citizenship. He asked: 'What does it mean to be Irish in this modern changing Ireland?'

> When it comes to identities: I grew up in Glasgow. I know what it means to be a Scottish Muslim of Pakistani descent. I have been to Belfast. I know Muslims in Northern Ireland, because there is a long history, there is a lot of discussion, a lot of debate about what British Muslim means, where it came from. I don't feel that being here in Cork. There's terms, there's phrases that I grew up with: We're all Jock Tamson's Bairns, Nicola Sturgeon says it all the time, it's not where you came from it's where we're going. I don't hear that in Ireland at all. All I hear is that we are the other. You're boxed in this very particular way. I don't hear this broad tent of Irishness and I'm still not hearing enough from our elected officials, our leaders at all.

He continued:

> I am a head of a department here at University College Cork, I have the privilege to help but I still don't feel a part of this society. I still don't feel a part of Ireland. And every single day I wake up and think, why do I not feel

that? So what does it mean to be Irish in 2021 in this modern changing Ireland?

The prevailing question now was not whether we can get rid of the border and assimilate the North. It was whether Ireland can assimilate migrants and accept them as neighbours.

Owodunni Ola Mustapha empathised with Amanullah De Sondy:

> The Ireland that the Irish people sell to us, the migrant community, is an Ireland of compassion, an Ireland of a thousand welcomes, an Ireland that is open to treating people in fairness which is also in the constitution of Ireland, but at every turn, in your journey in Ireland there is something or someone that still reminds you that your life is not complete, you're not part of us, you're never part of us, regardless of whether you speak the language. Regardless of whether you know the history of Ireland, there is still that someone, that clause or something that still reminds you that you are not fully Irish. I want to see an Ireland that I can get to live in and say that I am part of this society, part of something that brings a wholeness to my life and gives my children something to look up to and be proud of and I think that day will come. Change will come but it is always very slow in Ireland and I hope that we will all live to see that change manifest.

Then Karen Sethuraman joined in with more to say on this theme than she had been able to offer on the discussion around unification:

I am married to a guy from India and he has been here thirty years and we have three children and my daughter Megan last year shared with us her experience of racism, and when it comes into your home you realise we have a long way to go. She would say she's Irish and she took her Irish flag with her to university and she says the thing she always gets is, yes, you're Irish but you're not really from here.

Tadhg Hickey was surprised:

I wouldn't have thought that he [Amanullah De Sondy] felt that way. Sadly in the South we can be a country of othering. Ireland is also partitioned in terms of haves and have-nots. That's why we are here, to almost rip it up and start again and to listen to people where they feel excluded. I think it is a great point to make at the start of these conversations that it isn't all about constitutions and flags and Orange and Green and the ever-growing middle ground.

The point that had emerged most forcefully from the debate was that Ireland, the southern state, was damaged and had to fix itself. For republicans this raised the old historic question of whether reform can come before unity or if unity takes precedence among concerns.

One member of the audience said that a good starting point for putting things right would be the Proclamation of 1916 and the 1919 Declaration of Independence. Thomas Gould, a Sinn Féin TD for Cork North Central said:

If we adopt the attitude that a border poll must be put off until all issues are resolved that treats the aspirations of northern nationalists and those who in the North aspire to Irish unity as a lesser aspiration, then the status quo is somehow superior and I don't believe that can be the case. There is no doubt that the conversation will be difficult at times, but I do believe that the conversation is moving in that direction and I do believe that there is a wider acceptance in the North across nationalism and unionism than perhaps there is in the South at this point.

There is a balance to be struck and it needs to offer reassurance and stability, but it would be pointless if a united Ireland is not radically and substantially different. It has to offer something significantly new and something better.

But in the meantime, apparently, Amanullah De Sondy, Owodunni Ola Mustapha and Karen Sethuraman's daughter Megan would have to wait to be fully Irish until after nationalists in the North were.

Of course, there is no uniform Muslim or migrant view on whether or not Ireland can be one country. When Shaykh Dr Umar Al-Qadri of the Irish Muslim Peace and Integration Council joined the panel of another Ireland's Future meeting in the Mansion House in November, he urged unification for the sake of the beleaguered Muslims in 'the Six Counties'.

He said, 'In the twenty-six counties the Irish Muslim experience is one of the best if not the best in the whole of Europe. In the six counties however, the narrative is completely different. As nationalism becomes stronger, regressive elements within political unionism seek out new vulnerable targets, women, LGBTQI communities, disabled people, travellers, Muslims and other minorities.'

No one asked him to clarify who he was referring to as 'regressive elements within political unionism'. This was the problem with the whole meeting, there was no contention within it. The chairing by journalist Audrey Carville was effective mainly in terms of keeping people to time limits and expanding the range of discussion by raising questions about the economy and the preservation of the identity rights of unionists in the future new Ireland. But did anyone there seriously believe that members of unionist political parties or other organisations were deciding to beat up Muslims, gays and disabled people because nationalists are now too strong to be crossed?

Still, there are clear examples of abuse of Muslims and other ethnic minorities in Northern Ireland and Dr Al-Qadri presented an appalling example:

> In January this year [2021] the BMCA the Belfast Multicultural Association was burnt down in a horrific arson attack, which the PSNI described as a deliberate hate crime. BMCA was not just a mosque or an Islamic Centre. In fact the BMCA run a soup kitchen, they run a food bank, they provide essential support to frontline workers in the health service. They provided food parcels, running errands throughout the pandemic, but as of today the PSNI has made no arrests in connection with this horrific attack on not just a place of worship but

a focal point for the entire community. Such an attack would have been unthinkable in the twenty-six counties. And that for me is the crux of the issue.

He could have enriched his story further with the information that many in Northern Ireland were appalled by the attack on the BMCA. The leader of political unionism at the time, Arlene Foster, frankly condemned it. Amnesty International set up a crowdfunding appeal to help the BMCA to recover and handed over a cheque for £71,733 a month after the fire. So, while a small number of people attacked the building and the cars of staff there, many many more people than it would have taken to burn the place contributed money to restoring it. As a result it doesn't serve as a good illustration that Northern Ireland is generally hostile to Muslims.

However, the centre was attacked again in April 2022.

Dr Al-Qadri's endorsement of the 'twenty-six counties' as a welcoming place for Muslims has to be qualified by the comments made at the Cork meeting and by the European Islamophobia Report of 2018 (edited by Enes Bayrakli and Farid Hafez), which says, 'Ireland continues to see local and international fringe political actors undertake anti-Muslim activities.'

'Regressive elements' perhaps?

Dr Al-Qadri said:

Where there is such a difference between the lived experience of Muslim communities and on other minorities in the six and the twenty-six counties, political unionism should not be surprised when those communities reach the conclusion that despite having no historical or familial connection to the constitutional question, black people, people of colour, Muslims, LGBT and other non-traditional communities living in the North decide that partition is not working for them either. And to be blunt, political unionism is shooting itself in the foot here.

He argued that the outcome of a border poll is likely to be decided by middle-ground voters not attached to either of the traditional blocs and that that space is occupied by large numbers of migrants, new arrivals, people of colour: 'Having seen the differences between the experiences of my community in the twenty-six counties and my community in the six counties, I say proudly that I believe in a united Ireland. I pray for a united Ireland. By God, I am willing to work to deliver a united Ireland.'

On the panel that day also was Professor John Doyle, who argued that a united Ireland was economically viable. He rejected the standard argument that the £10 billion subvention from the British exchequer was clear evidence of unity being too expensive: 'If the Northern Ireland economy was equivalent to the average in the Republic there wouldn't be a subvention.' Part of that subvention covered costs that would not have to be met by Ireland, like the contribution to the British defence budget. Indeed, the need for a subvention was evidence of the economic failure of Northern Ireland, which could be put right with unification.

The problem was, 'the gap in higher education, the gap in finishing school. It's the gap in investment and tourism.' He said investors 'are not going to Northern Ireland. It's two hours up the road. Why? Rents are cheaper, wages are cheaper. It's about political instability, it's about the future, it's about Brexit now.

Let's not get fixated on the subvention, which is an historic legacy of economic weakness.'

A report of the Independent Fiscal Commission NI, published in December 2021, put the annual figure for money paid by the British Exchequer to Northern Ireland at £14.8 billion. This includes taxation raised in Northern Ireland for which no clear figure seems available. In a paper published around the same time, Professor Doyle said that pension costs were 'unlikely to be transferred'. In other words, after the unification of Ireland, Britain would continue to pay the pensions of those of us who have been paying national insurance contributions all our lives into a notional pension pot:

> Many Irish citizens, in retirement in Ireland, receive their UK pension seamlessly, and the two tax and social welfare systems have a well-developed model of cooperation. It seems consistent that the UK would pay pension liability that had been built up, based on individuals' tax and social insurance contributions or caring responsibilities, during Northern Ireland's membership of the United Kingdom. (Doyle, 2021, p. 323.)

He calculated that Northern Irish pension payments (including my own) amount to about £3.5 billion a year.

Professor Doyle's assumption that Britain would continue to pay the pensions bill was debunked by Newton Emerson in one of his regular columns in *The Irish Times*, on 10 February 2022, who argued that there is no 'pension pot' preserving national insurance contributions accumulated over the decades and that Scottish nationalists had already dropped the idea that an independent Scotland would not be responsible for continuing payments. He cited what he called the 'expat fallacy', which compares countries that leave the UK to pensioners who retire abroad and still draw their British pensions. 'But such people do not take a chunk of the UK and its tax base with them.'

Alan Barrett of the Economic and Social Research Institute argued in reply to Doyle that the very danger that a deal made with Ireland would have to be replicated with Scotland makes it much more likely that Britain would resist having to pay the pensions of former British citizens in a united Ireland. That imagines Ireland uniting before Scotland leaves the UK, but presumably if Scotland goes first, it will set the precedent for how Northern Ireland's exit from the UK might be managed. And the far larger Scottish economy would require more stringent negotiation. So the prospect of Scottish independence may actually cast a shadow over the prospects of Irish unity rather than be the stimulus many see it as.

Mary Lou McDonald, who was also part of the panel at the November meeting, said that the economic argument for unity was 'a slam dunk'. Like all the speakers there, she made the argument that unity was practical and necessary. She also wanted to establish continuity in the least contentious way between the rebels of 1916 and the panel she was sitting on:

> While I never argue that we should be captive to our past because our job is to write our present and to imagine our future and to deliver it, we should be conscious that we meet in a place where a century ago, brave women – more brave men sadly than women – met and imagined

a new tomorrow, asked themselves the question that we now are faced with in our generation: what country do we want? What country can we have and what country can we share?

But she said nothing about fulfilling the aspirations of Patrick Pearse. The Proclamation didn't get a mention.

> I believe that we should frame this conversation in the language of opportunity not fear, not winners and losers, not any zero sum game but an opportunity for all of us in which each has a voice and none has a veto … nobody is handing down a new Ireland on tablets of stone to the populace. As the leader of Sinn Féin, and the republican movement, I am not doing that. That frankly is not my job.

I had thought that that was precisely what her job was, as leader of a movement that traces its lineage back to the Provisional Government. Apparently not.

Fianna Fáil's Jim O'Callaghan was emphatic that unification was not about healing the injustices of the past but about creating a new country that would be 'a shining beacon to the world':

> The real reason to vote for Irish unification is that it would transform the island and it would create a new country in which there would be greater opportunities for people living in both jurisdictions. It would create a stronger country that would have much more influence

throughout the world. It would create a country with a much bigger economy that would increase the standard of living for everybody on the island. It would create a country with a much more diverse population. One of the criticisms of the two jurisdictions is that we had very limited diversity. But it would also be a shining beacon to the world of what can be achieved through reconciliation and agreement.

It would surely, if agreement could be reached.

At this meeting, Neale Richmond was the nearest they got to a unionist on the panel. The Fine Gael TD for Dublin Rathdown, he has Protestant relations in the North and said that his forebears were more likely to have been shooting into the GPO than shooting out of it. Richmond wants a united Ireland and he wants the unionists to stay so that he can go on enjoying large family gatherings at Christmas:

It's not going to be a state that's all about Brits Out. I fundamentally believe it's going to be a state that's about Brits In. There are 300,000 British citizens who live in this jurisdiction and nearly one million British citizens who live in the North. I don't want anyone of a unionist persuasion or other to feel that they have to leave a united Ireland. I want them to stay. This is their country as much as it is our country. And we will respect their identity.

But they were not part of the discussion. Many have been invited and have refused to participate. There was no one to ask, let alone answer, how to assure unionists of a British identity while depriving them of British citizenship.

I have been a little wry in my northerner's evaluation of these debates and I have tended, perhaps, to shed light on the most glaringly superficial and trite comments, like Mary Lou McDonald's assertion that loyalists in east Belfast are clamouring to learn Irish, Tadhg Hickey's claim that the nationalists in the North are stateless, Karen Sethuraman's insistence that we ask the children. But perhaps the quality of the debate on unification being so poor suggests that there should be more of it rather than less.

14

THOSE TO BE PERSUADED

THERE SHOULD HAVE been an empty seat at the Ireland's Future events for a northern unionist. In fact, there should probably have been three or four, for unionism is not a monolithic force such as it once was. The spectrum of unionism ranges from people who would not apply the word to themselves, who perhaps do not vote for any party but who would rather stay within the UK, to those who, like the late Rev. Ian Paisley, believe that Ulster is Protestant and must remain so, the only guarantor of their freedom being the Protestant faith and the British monarchy.

To be fair, there are few who would take their stand on that latter position today, though it was a major political force just a generation ago. And it might be hard to find someone to represent the former position, since it is essentially apathetic.

I'll start with myself.

I would describe myself at times as a small u unionist and at other times as a small n nationalist. I am no asset to any unionist party, though I have occasionally given an Ulster Unionist a second preference vote to hold back other candidates I liked less.

I might vote against unification, depending on the deal on offer and the circumstances of the time. The pension question will be critical. IF is right to say that we need to know what the deal will be before a vote, but there is no requirement in the Good Friday Agreement for Britain to set out terms or negotiate with anyone before calling a referendum.

I am neither an ideological unionist nor a principled nationalist. Such ambivalence would have appalled or at least bemused my father. My mother, whose own mother was a secretary in the British Legion, might have been more sympathetic. I am at the most remote fringe of unionist thinking, wary of the British Army, contemptuous of the British monarchy. I have several times been asked to speak to army officers and have travelled to Germany to address seminars, yet once the man who was delegated to pay me at the end of an event turned up in uniform and I reflexively stepped back from him.

If I was to join even the more moderate UUP, I would find myself in meeting rooms with a portrait of the Queen on the wall, the Union flag in a corner and several other reminders of British Ulster ethnicity. Unionism is a culture, not just an ideology, and I would not be at ease within it.

I have a Protestant friend who felt a similar distancing of herself when she joined the SDLP, attended a party conference and then found herself at a breakfast table in the conference hotel being asked which Mass she was going to.

A little further along from my place at the extreme end of the unionist spectrum we would find Sorcha Eastwood. Sorcha is a member of the Alliance Party. She is a Catholic, or at least was raised one and was educated in Catholic schools. She grew up on a farm near the garrison town of Lisburn and went to a Catholic primary school, St Joseph's. She recalls, 'I was in P7 at the time of the Drumcree thing and half the class were drawing

Union Jacks and the other half were drawing tricolours. Half their parents were RUC or prison service. They weren't Protestant.'

The 'Drumcree thing' was a spate of rioting across Northern Ireland in support of or opposing the right of an Orange Parade from Drumcree church in Portadown to march through the predominantly Catholic Garvaghy Road.

Sorcha says that soldiers were around her in a relaxed and friendly way when she was a child and she acquired the easy habit of assuming that they were friendly and supportive.

When older she went to St Dominic's, a girls' grammar school on the Falls Road. There, other girls saw her as a Protestant because of her accent and the fact that she was from Lisburn. 'Then I had to get the bus home where there are boys from Inst and Methody, girls from Victoria, because I didn't get the normal bus that went to Lisburn through Andytown. I had to get out to the bottom of the road from Great Victoria Street on the Banbridge bus.'

Northern Ireland is so divided territorially that Protestant and Catholic school children go home in different directions on different buses. She was the exception, a Catholic girl in a Catholic school uniform on a bus used mostly by children from Protestant schools. 'And I was called a Fenian, a taig, was spat on. Yet inside school I was a Prod. How does that make any sense?'

Catholic girls from west Belfast assumed from her accent and background that she could not possibly be a Catholic like themselves. In a way they were right, for she did not share their aversion to the police and the state.

One day the President of Ireland, Mary McAleese, came to visit her school. She was a former pupil. The RUC was there to protect her. Sorcha remembers, 'We were in the music room when her big entourage arrived and the girls got up and started singing SS RUC out the windows, so I was never more mortified in my life. Gerry Adams turned up. He said, *Dia duit*. I thought, *Get away from me.*'

Adams would have judged by her name that she was a proud Gael, but she says her mother called her Sorcha because she thought it was Russian. Her discomfort in a Gaelic context and her refusal to identify as a nationalist or unionist is what led her to the Alliance Party, which takes no formal position on the border. It seeks to bring both communities together to govern Northern Ireland without life being disrupted by divisions over the constitution. She says that she finds southern politicians patronising and superficial in their grasp of the complexities of Northern Ireland. 'I don't care who you are, if you are not doing right by this place and if you are not prepared to listen to us and what we are actually saying, I'll call you out.'

She recalled for me the experience of giving evidence at an Oireachtas Committee on the Good Friday Agreement:

> It rapidly turned into: Oh, we've a unionist here and a Shinner here and isn't that lovely, shake hands and be friends and it will all be grand.
>
> And I was just like, are you joking?
>
> I couldn't help myself. I said, I understand what you are saying on one level, but you've got to understand that a lot of people in Northern Ireland don't regard themselves as either unionist or nationalist and they have already made that journey themselves, either

because they've had to or for most of them because they want to. And as for this idea of Northern Ireland being 'solved' if a unionist and a nationalist talk to each other and isn't that fantastic, don't patronise.

Her Uncle Eamon joined us for a chat on the farm. It was interesting to watch Sorcha respond to some of the things he said. He had memories of the Troubles from before she was born. Their farm is close to the Maze Prison and after the big breakout of 1983, frantic armed soldiers invaded the farm looking for escaped prisoners and weren't at all civil about it. He believes one of them came close to shooting him, convinced he was providing shelter to the IRA.

Eamon thinks his future is in the Union. He says: 'I don't think for one minute that the South of Ireland wants us. Anybody who is fighting for a united Ireland is somebody who has never worked down there. They've been down in Bundoran for a week's holiday and think they know all about it.'

I say to Sorcha, aren't you essentially a unionist?

'I don't think so, no.'

But Eamon says, 'I think we are. We were brought up unionist. We had our health service, we had our jabs before anybody else. I'm not saying I'm a unionist in a political sense but in economical terms.'

Sorcha says, 'We are all very much Labour and I just think everybody just wants Labour to succeed. I have absolutely no problem with the monarchy. I have put people forward for OBEs and MBEs and I know how much it means to them.'

She doesn't believe that either London or Dublin can prioritise concerns about Northern Ireland. 'They will always put their own concerns first. The best people to speak for us are our own.'

A little further along the spectrum, perhaps towards the middle, is Trevor Ringland. He remembers a time living in west Belfast before the Troubles. His father was a policeman. 'Life was normal. Your neighbours were your neighbours. You were no better off than them nor worse off than them, and there was absolutely no threat in any shape or form to our lives at that time. We left before the Troubles.'

Trevor says he was part of a group of six police families who went down to Arklow for summer holidays in the sixties and had a wonderful time. He played rugby. 'That was an all-Ireland sport. I could play for the province of Ulster against Munster, Leinster and Connaught and then combine with them to take on England, Scotland, Wales and France. And then again we'd combine as the British and Irish Lions and take on the southern hemisphere.'

There is a softness of manner about Trevor that is hard for me to translate into an image of him charging down a field with a ball and shouldering challengers out of his way before diving headlong into the grass. He was for a time a member of the UUP, but fell out with them because he wanted the new party leader, Tom Elliott, to attend a GAA match, something he had said before his elevation to the leadership in 2010 that he would not do.

Trevor said:

> I said I would guarantee him that if there is an Ulster team in the All-Ireland final I would get him two tickets for that final.

I wanted to hear him say that if I got him those tickets that he would go to that match. Because I saw people who are reaching out to the unionist community, reaching out to try and build a shared society here and they needed encouragement as well. They needed to see and hear a unionism that actually wants to have a relationship with them.

He was accused of naivety and not taking into account that GAA finals were played on a Sunday. Many Protestants follow the tradition of avoiding work and play on the sabbath.

Trevor Ringland is now a member of the Northern Ireland conservatives. He is a solicitor and has an MBE for services to the community. Does he think Ireland can be one country?

I think Ireland is one in a whole lot of different ways that some people tend to ignore. It is also divided and there are good reasons for that. I take a broad-brush approach and say it's because we got relationships wrong and that had a consequence. If we have learnt anything over the years, it's that you can be together even though you are separate and that is probably okay.

We have to look and see where we got those relationships wrong and it is incumbent on us to try and get them right in the future. How do we look after all our children so that they succeed? And how others' children do is as important to me as how my own do. In that way we should all do well.

For him one of the divisive elements is a strong republican

tradition which endorses the IRA campaign: 'As somebody who is unionist, pro-union Ulster Scots, Northern Irish, from a police family, then I wonder why it is that half the population would think a campaign of violence that was really about removing me from this island and people like me is somehow justified and okay.'

He knows that if the IRA had blown up his father with a bomb under his car, and with him as a child sitting beside him, that there are still many people in political life in Ireland who would remember that as, at worst, a sad inevitability, and who would commemorate the bomber as a hero if, by chance, he too had died in the blast.

He is a believer in the prospects of ending sectarianism and having good relations between communities in the North inside the Union and good relations between the two parts of Ireland without political unification. He recalls how Northern Ireland soccer had been toxically sectarian until it recognised that it was damaging itself by accommodating bigotry: 'They had deteriorated to a place where the atmosphere was horrendous, deeply sectarian, unfamily-friendly and the crowds had dropped to five or six thousand for a World Cup qualifier. You could see that the team was uncomfortable being out on the pitch to the extent that I said I would not go back.'

A friend who was from a nationalist background urged him to stay on as a fan on the logic that if those offended by the bigotry left then only the bigots themselves would remain. In time, a community relations officer was appointed to work with the fans and get them to see the damage their sectarianism was doing to the game:

They looked at themselves and they said, what are we like? And they thought, well actually we are pretty horrible. We're alienating people from the game. We're destroying the thing we love so we need to change, and they sought ideas and constructive criticism from critical friends from all backgrounds and new songs. The red, white and blue from the terraces went to a sea of green, the green and white army. They used loudhailers to drown out those who tried to sing sectarian songs. They self-disciplined. You hear stories now that if they are on a tour somewhere and some of the fans start singing the old songs, the old guys go up to them and say, son, we don't do that any more. And the family friendly atmosphere is back.

But crucially, this liberal, anti-sectarian unionism, this most honestly self-reflective and generous unionism, is still unionism:

My unionism is not up for negotiation. A major part of unionism is they love Ireland. That's a good place to start. They love this part of Ireland and they see it as their home. They want to share it. The province of Ulster is different because of the Scottish influence. I think with my family name there is an English input but on my mother's side there would be that Scottish influence as well.

What was her name? She was a Kerr from Fermanagh, the same name as my Irish-speaking grandmother from the neighbouring county, Donegal.

The Kerrs originated in the Scottish borders, so my granny had Planter forebears. The border has failed to divide Planters and Gaels, and if we were to try to create such a border, where would we put it? We have contrived one, that's what sectarianism is – but even a mental, notional abstract border can't exist without cutting through families and people.

I say to Trevor, you would still have the Scottish strand of culture in the North after unification. Belfast won't be shipped down South. The same geographical and cultural connections will still be there. It is surely only a question of administration. He says:

> I can enjoy that all-Ireland aspect of it as well. That is part of who I am too. I have three English nephews and three English nieces and two English brothers-in-law and a Scottish nephew and niece. I like being part of a country that has the Commonwealth, such a lovely organisation, all these countries and the smallest is equal with the biggest, India with some small Caribbean island and that is such a part of our history. It's the sense of inclusion. Go to London and see the place that it is. It's a world city.

He would rather Britain had stayed in the EU, but he worried also about the European concept of ever closer union stirring up nationalistic responses. 'Look at what happened to Yugoslavia.'

As for the monarchy, he says it is not crucial to his sense of being British, but he prefers monarchy to a presidential system:

> If your country goes to war often the children of the monarch go to war. That's not always the case with the

politicians who send you to war. The sense of stability that they have in that means we can now look forward to nearly another seventy-five years of who is going to be in place, whereas in the presidential system I see more egos.

It's more the concept of an inclusive country and a country that is able to accommodate diversity. And the economic factors are there as well. We are part of UK PLC. We give some of our best talent to drive that economy. It's the simple fact that I feel safe and secure inside the UK.

This inclusiveness is exactly what Ireland's Future and people like Matthew O'Toole on the New Ireland Commission say they aspire to. Trevor sees that the greater inclusiveness would be within the UK, which is already far more diverse than Ireland is ever likely to be.

I ask him if he worries about demographic change in Northern Ireland. A time will come when the bred-in-the-blood unionists of the Protestant and Scots tradition will not be in a majority and will not be able to preserve the Union without the support of many others. Those others may be persuaded to vote against a united Ireland on pragmatic grounds, but they will not have that same heartfelt attachment to Britain. They will be Irish people voting to stay outside Ireland. Isn't that a lot to ask of them? Does he not feel that a Union depending on their commitment would be insecure? He says:

If we get it right, this place will do well. If we look around the world, we appreciate this place more for what it gives us. Most of us want a politics that takes responsibility and looks to shape the place in a way that we all enjoy and do well in. If we are creating somewhere that is ours, all of us who live here, which we all want to feel is our shared home place, then that's a good thing.

I ask him if he is not responding more to Sinn Féin and the hurt caused by the IRA campaign than to the prospect of a new Ireland, which need not be nearly as alienating of Protestants and British-identifying people as it clearly was in the past.

Willie Redmond said you may woo us into a united Ireland, but you cannot coerce us. You can never say never to anything, but if you are wanting to marry someone do you buy them chocolates and dinners and tell them they are looking well or do you hit them?

Why would they want to unite with a group of people they don't like? Is it the place they are after, not the people? It is so incredibly difficult to undo the damage of violence.

*

Another plainly anti-sectarian unionist is Doug Beattie, leader of the UUP at the time of writing. The party has been through rapid leadership changes in recent years.

This was the historic unionist party of James Craig, the first prime minister of Northern Ireland. It was the party of Lord Brookeborough, who famously said he wouldn't have a Catholic about the place; of Terence O'Neill, who pleaded with the Civil Rights campaigners to give him a bit more time; of Brian Faulkner, who introduced internment of republican suspects in 1971 and two years later agreed to share power with the SDLP, having signed up to what would be the first draft of the Good Friday Agreement. He was brought down by the Ulster Workers' Council Strike of 1974. This was also the party of David Trimble, who led his people back into talks, assented to the Good Friday Agreement in 1998 and was later sidelined by Rev. Ian Paisley's DUP.

Doug Beattie is the latest in a line of unionist leaders seeking to recover ground from the DUP. He wants to establish a unionism which extends beyond Protestantism and wins over some who might otherwise vote for a united Ireland by persuading them that they can be comfortably at home in Northern Ireland. A big fellow, and a lot more gregarious than Trevor Ringland, his first career was in the military. His mother died when he was fourteen and he joined up at sixteen with no qualifications. He served in Bosnia, in Iraq and Afghanistan.

He is frank about having killed there, once with a bayonet in hand-to-hand combat in Helmand:

> I am not proud of it, but he was trying to kill me and that is what I had. So that whole brutality of conflict affects you, and you try to explain to people as I explain it now and it is hard to explain what it is like because when you are in Afghanistan in the middle of that environment, doing what you are doing, it is impossible to think of yourself walking through Tesco and when you are walking through Tesco it is really impossible to think of yourself in Afghanistan doing that very thing. So you have to try and understand that feeling, but you lose it when you leave the environment. It was pretty brutal.

I wondered if having killed made it easier for him to empathise with former IRA members who had killed or tried to kill and were now politicians he worked with. He says:

> I look at them and I think, whatever you thought you were doing for the good of whoever, whether your cause was a united Ireland or to stay in the United Kingdom, what you did was absolutely counterproductive. It left this country bleeding and grieving for many years. And that is why I sit now and say we cannot repeat that failure.
>
> That's why I look to those people who had that failure twenty or thirty years ago to be the ones to step forward and say, we got it wrong so don't follow us.

Doug says some loyalists own up to having taken the wrong course, but republicans don't. He also accepts that the days of Protestant unionism are over. He has never been a member of the Orange Order, though until recent times it was unthinkable that his party would be led by someone who didn't march on the Twelfth of July to commemorate the Battle of the Boyne.

His father wouldn't allow talk about religion at home and he didn't know he was a Protestant until he was ten years old, but it's not even clear that he is a Protestant, if that word describes a theology and practice. He doesn't go to church:

> I have a belief. I slept in a half-dug grave in Garmsir in Afghanistan. A Muslim graveyard. And it was brutal. Some of the things that I was seeing and doing I never expected to see or do in my lifetime, and I was coming to

my forties and I reached out to God within that trench, lying there alone and saying, please help me stay alive; please help me keep my soldiers alive. Please help us get out of here. And I felt a real sense of something coming in. And that spiritual feeling, I hold that very dear and very close to me and very private to me. I don't need to express that in a church.

He does not appeal exclusively to a Protestant electorate as his predecessors would have done. He knows that if he doesn't cater to some extent for the younger more secular part of the electorate he will lose them to other parties. They are most likely to turn to the Alliance Party, which refuses to designate as unionist or nationalist and has a rapidly growing support base for the politics of putting the constitutional question aside. Doug Beattie won't put it aside, but neither will he engage with Ireland's Future and its campaign to widen discussion on what a united Ireland would be like.

He describes himself as a constitutional unionist:

The union will ebb and flow. It goes through good times and bad times. It has good governments and bad governments. In the same way, Ireland is really on the up, but they'll hit a peak. There is ebb and flow in all of society. But the Union is important as the fifth largest global economy in the world. Its position in the world, notwithstanding who's in charge at the moment, has been overwhelmingly positive. Take conflicts out of it.

I thought he would say something like: 'You don't ask a French person why she doesn't want to be German, so why are you puzzled that I don't want to be Irish.' But he says he is Irish.

I asked him: 'What are the elements of the Union that are important to you? The monarchy?'

> Yes, the monarchy is important to me but it's the Union itself that people don't get. The fundamental is that I as an Irishman – I have always classed myself as Irish – can stand in Scotland and be uniquely Irish and feel at home. And I can live in England, as I have done, and be uniquely Irish and feel at home. Or Wales.
>
> And I have lived and worked and had a house in those three countries.
>
> I feel less at home in Dublin or Galway, slightly apart when I go down there, but I am also tied in because culturally a lot of what we have, we have in common. I think structurally the two parts of this island have become slightly different. That's why it has become a slight place apart.
>
> But standing with somebody from Dublin or Galway, as I have done, in the deserts of Afghanistan, I felt as Irish as they did. Actually, as a people, when taken away from that geographical space, we have an awful lot in common.
>
> This is home. Everything changes. Society moves on. I will get old. I will die. My kids will get old. They will die. I want to remain part of the United Kingdom. I believe I will be part of the United Kingdom for the whole of my life. I believe that my kids will be in the United Kingdom for the whole of their lives.

He will campaign for the Union in a border poll if it comes, but he sounds as if he would adapt easily to whatever came out of it: 'If we were ever to have a united Ireland, be that a united Ireland as part of the UK or a united Ireland completely separate within the EU, it is still my home, the people are still my people, either side of the border.'

I got a similar feeling from Trevor Ringland and Sorcha Eastwood – that they are provisional unionists, more committed to peace and stability than to asserting a British identity. For people like these it is inconceivable that they would use violence to assert or defend the Union in any circumstance short of Irish army tanks roaring in, or even then. But they will not be put to that test anyway. Doug himself says:

> I would not take up a weapon to defend the Union. I have heard some who would, but I wouldn't. I know what conflict is. I know what it will do and what it will not do. We can make our case politically to stay part of the United Kingdom. That's what we should focus on.
>
> Whether we should be doing it today, now, I don't think we need to. There's time to do that at the right time. I don't think anyone is making sensible arguments. I think there is a lot of great words and rhetoric going round. I am a democrat so I would support democratically whatever the outcome of the poll would be. I sometimes do wish that other people would be as democratic in their acceptance of other votes. If the island is to be unified, then it will be unified and I will stay here and live here.

But he will not plan for that because he does not expect it to happen. And he has a message for Ireland's Future: 'Why would I give you the solutions to the problems that you have? Why would I design something for you when I don't want it? It doesn't make sense. Have your conversations. Come up with your plan. Put your plan on the table and then let people choose.'

But couldn't a strong unionist voice deal with some of the naivety coming across in the discussions? Like that claim by Mary Lou McDonald that the people of east Belfast are 'voting with their feet' in a clamour to learn the Irish language; or Tadhg Hickey's claim that the Irish in the North have been deserted, speak better Irish than they do in the South and fly tricolours from their windows. Couldn't someone have been in Cork to answer that woman who said she doesn't understand why anyone in the North would want to be part of the UK? When Shaykh Dr Umar Al-Qadri said that 'regressive elements of political unionism' were now turning on Muslims, gays and the disabled, would it not have been helpful if someone had asked him who he was talking about? Where is this political unionism that is now cowering from confronting nationalism and lashing out at migrants and people in wheelchairs?

At another meeting in Galway in October 2021, Sinn Féin TD Mairéad Farrell said she thought the Irish language was a 'commonality' that the people of Ireland might be united by. There was no one there to tell her that the language is one of the key things nationalists and unionists are divided on. But Doug Beattie says, 'People who are attending these meetings are people who want a united Ireland so anything that I say as a unionist will make no difference.'

And he actually takes confidence from the rise of Sinn Féin in the republic:

> There is a fundamental change coming about. Sinn Féin is going to be the government in the Irish Republic. That's going to end the united Ireland debate for a five-year period because even some of the strongest nationalists who want a united Ireland but who will not ever support Sinn Féin will not be in that camp. Sinn Féin in government in the Irish Republic is one of our strongest assets.

But there could be a situation soon where Mary Lou McDonald is the Taoiseach, and she and Michelle O'Neill will be meeting at cross-border bodies and having summits. That will look to the naive like a united Ireland already. That suggestion doesn't impress him: 'The reality will still be exactly the same and that is we'll still be part of the United Kingdom.'

Doug Beattie is exuding a confidence that a united Ireland is simply not likely in his lifetime. Some unionists refused to even discuss the matter with me on the grounds that I was in danger of making the prospect plausible. They do not want to be part of a discussion premised on the ultimate inevitability of Irish unity. That may be their strategic response to those who insist that unity is coming. They simply want to project a similar confidence that it isn't.

Or maybe they are right.

15

CAN IRELAND BE TWO?

IF IRELAND CANNOT be one, can it be two?

There is no doubt that the Protestant/unionist people of the northeast of the island do regard themselves as distinct, a population with a core ethnic identity and with an ambition to remain separate from the Irish state. The parameters of that identity sometimes seem not to be very sharp. Doug Beattie and Mervyn Gibson assert their Irishness while wanting to belong to a British jurisdiction. Many Protestants now vote for the Alliance Party, which is officially agnostic on Irish unity. But at its core, this identity is solid and convincing. And a sense of being Irish for these people doesn't rival their Britishness in any meaningful way.

The partition of Ireland was an attempt to accommodate that identity, providing unionists with autonomy while creating an Irish Free State for those who adamantly insisted on being Irish. It was not a perfect solution for it divided both those British and Irish communities too, cutting off minorities from the state created for the benefit of their people. A Protestant minority got stuck in the South and a Catholic minority in the North.

Unionists before partition had talked of Ulster as their

homeland. The war cry of unionism before partition – Ulster will fight and Ulster will be right – implied loyalty to the whole province. Orangemen had rallied in the nineteenth century to protest Catholic Association activity in Monaghan. Discussions on how a border might be drawn had first contemplated the inclusion of Monaghan, Cavan and Donegal, parts of the province of Ulster that had substantial Protestant minorities. Some have argued that had unionists started out by trying to calculate how much space they could reasonably expect to hold in perpetuity and seeking to have it integrated into the UK rather than having power devolved to it, they might have been more secure and at peace for much longer.

The identification of Northern Ireland as Ulster is still retained in the naming of Ulster Television, Radio Ulster, the University of Ulster, the Ulster Unionist Party, the Ulster Volunteer Force, the Ulster Hospital, the Royal Ulster Academy and more. This retention of the Ulster title is a remnant of a forgotten hope that the entire province might be a homeland for unionists, detached from the rest of Ireland.

When partition was contemplated as a compromise short of Home Rule, unionists understood that they could not govern Monaghan, Cavan and Donegal, and that six counties were as much as was practicable for them to hold. They were still seeking to maximise the territory they could claim, some thinking that they could succeed in withdrawing enough land from the rest of Ireland to make their neighbours' territory unviable. Some considered at least bringing Donegal into a seven-county 'Ulster', creating a more defensible border from east coast to west coast, from Warrenpoint to just south of Bundoran. That was thinking that anticipated war.

Oliver MacDonagh wonders why the new entity should have been composed of counties, when deciding its shape and size by parliamentary constituencies might have produced 'a much finer measure' (1983, p. 22). Then, South Armagh, South Down, South Fermanagh and most of Tyrone would have gone to the Free State, as also might Derry city have done. Some of those areas became the most difficult to cope with during the Troubles. If partition might have worked better had the line been drawn more carefully, might we now be ready to consider redrawing the border and providing unionists with a smaller state in which they would be more secure?

This idea cropped up from time to time, but the modern European political mind is not keen on creating ethnically pure states. At least two British prime ministers during the Troubles period considered repartitioning Northern Ireland and handing a chunk of it over to the Republic. Edward Heath commissioned a report in the early 1970s into whether a revised partition and the relocation of Catholics would resolve the difficulties of the time and placate the IRA. That report is now accessible through the Public Records Office and the CAIN website, and it reads like an eloquent dismissal through irrefutable logic of an idea that appalled the author. Margaret Thatcher took advice on the idea too, and aired it with her diplomats in the negotiations leading to the Anglo-Irish Agreement of 1985.

Heath, in wondering if repartition might work, understood that it would trap disgruntled minorities again unless there were enforced population transfers across the new border. A major and obvious practical difficulty with repartition would be the question of how to divide Belfast and draw the new border round half of it. Could Catholic west Belfast be linked to the Republic through a land corridor? The M1 motorway would be handy in this respect. And the city is already divided by peace walls and the River Lagan. Didn't West Berlin have a land corridor to West Germany? Yet that is hardly the sort of analogy that would sell repartition to a British or Irish government.

Every argument for how repartition might be made to work quickly becomes an explanation for why it cannot possibly be done. But to argue that repartition is a hopeless and unjust solution amounts to an acknowledgement that partition was wrong in the first place.

There is a roughly definable unionist territory. It has shrunk since partition, back from the border to the River Bann and probably further back still. It covers much of Counties Antrim and Down and an area south of Lough Neagh. Unionism, being geographically located will, even in a united Ireland, retain local government authority over specific areas and stamp its character upon them.

The idea of redrawing boundaries and even shifting populations seems a simple and obvious solution, since it is just a refinement of what was done before at partition. If you defend partition, how can you argue against repartition? You can do it because the world has changed. Heath and Thatcher's dalliances with the idea came before the Balkan wars gave us the term 'ethnic cleansing', but, in Heath's case, just twenty-five years after the partition of India and the driving of Palestinians from their homes to create the state of Israel. He should have known from his own experience of war and its aftermath that population transfers require trains and transit camps and cost a lot of lives. The horror is that he had to have the reality spelled out for him, leaving us with a document in which an official, in the tones of a patient teacher, explains what a horribly bad idea repartition is.

A draft of the document (reference: PREM 15/1010, 22 July 1972) is stamped Top Secret above and below the main text. It reads: 'We have been asked to consider whether it would be practicable to move the dissident republican population out of Northern Ireland retaining only the Unionist population.'

Part of this first paragraph that I have just quoted is actually written on the document in pen to replace scored-out typed copy which puts the case more starkly: 'A course which has not yet been studied in detail, and which may appear to be in harmony with the military operation preceding the conference, is to move the dissident republican population out of the United Kingdom, retaining only the unionist population.'

The difference between the two versions suggests that the idea was originally approached with some hope of it being viable, while the penned version adopts a flatter tone that raises no expectation of a credible plan. The only reason the author is considering it is because 'We have been asked …' The implication is that, had they not been asked, they would never have bothered their heads with such a barbarous idea.

The conference referred to in the typed print was the Darlington Conference of 1972, which opened the way to the Sunningdale talks and the first power-sharing experiment a year later. Heath was trying to persuade nationalist parties to take part in the conference, something they would refuse to do. He was perhaps thinking, absurdly, that that difficulty would be overcome if he shifted all of their voters out of their homes and into another jurisdiction.

This is how the practical difficulties were laid out in civil service language:

> Though Republicanism is often equated with Roman Catholicism, the two terms by no means cover the same ground. Many Catholics prefer the union with Great Britain; and many more feel only an emotional attraction to the Republican ideal. No accurate and recent polls are available; a 1968 poll suggested that only one Catholic in three favoured a united Ireland, and a recent small sample poll pointed to similar conclusions. Nevertheless in the absence of any better guide to political sympathies the following paragraphs assume that the Catholic minority are to be removed from Northern Ireland.

In other words, we may have to shift about three times as many people as required to make the plan work since we don't have time to ask all Catholics where their loyalties lie. People were therefore to have their citizenship revoked and be expelled from the state on religious grounds. That would not have been a good look on the global scene, though it would have gladdened the heart of the most caustic sectarian Protestant bigot.

The report also considered the transfer of territory from Northern Ireland to the Republic, a redrawing of the border. It could not consider appropriating territory from the Republic. 'In considering the transfer of territory, first consideration would be given to hiving off those areas with a simple Catholic majority at the most recent census. (To conduct a fresh plebiscite for the purpose of obtaining the majority view in each area would be to invite delay and chaos in the areas involved.)' Clearly what was being contemplated was not a long-term plan to reshape Northern Ireland but an imminent large-scale shifting of populations, 'in harmony with the military operation'.

The maps of the areas to be handed over to the Republic are very rough, just broad curves through Counties Fermanagh and Down and a small, shaded area around Ballycastle on the northeast coast. There is no finesse to the drawing, presumably because the author already understands that a more detailed map will not be needed.

According to the report's author:

Such a scheme would have a number of flaws:

(i) It would create enclaves of Republican territory within Northern Ireland and Northern enclaves in the Republic.

(ii) It would transfer nearly as many Protestants as Catholics.

(iii) It would ignore the much larger Catholic population (284,000) who live in local authority areas where they are not in the majority.

(iv) It would transfer some areas that are electorally Unionist.

Quoting from this amazing report is probably more effective than paraphrasing it, for it displays the cold reasoning of officials who had taken their brief seriously and treated the option of repartition as plausible, while comprehensively demolishing it:

The ceding of part of the United Kingdom would raise obvious political difficulties, but quite apart from these, land transfer alone would not succeed in removing the dissidents. People would have to be moved as well. This too would raise formidable difficulties. Assuming it were undertaken in conjunction with a land transfer – the Republic would surely not accept 500,000 Catholics without land for them to live on – there would be a need to remove 200,000–300,000 Catholics from other parts of Northern Ireland into the ceded areas; and to bring up 200,000 Protestants out of the ceded areas into the remainder of Northern Ireland.

So, they would hand over responsibility for Newry and Derry and big chunks of Tyrone and South Armagh to the Republic. They would move Catholics into those areas from other parts of Northern Ireland and move Protestants out of those areas into the homes from which the Catholics had been extracted.

This was not going to be easy. It would require the assent and cooperation of the Irish government. No consideration was given to moving Protestants out of the Republic, other than the ceded areas, into the smaller Northern Ireland. Moving Irish citizens would not have been within the power of the British government and would have had no relevance to the military objective of depriving the IRA of territory in Northern Ireland from which to operate.

About one third of the population of Northern Ireland would be on the move. Such a massive move would not be peacefully accomplished; great resistance could be expected from many of those who should move. The Catholics would face initial homelessness and unemployment (since they would outnumber the spaces left by the Protestants) and reduced social services, and all would face prolonged uncertainty and upheaval.

Nor would those forced to move be happy to go just because they were helping to bring stability that they themselves had not threatened: 'Many would no doubt take the view that they should not be the ones to pay the price for peace in Northern Ireland: Catholics demanding justice where they were, and refusing to become refugees to obtain it, and Protestants seeing the need to move as poor reward for their "loyalty" to the Crown.'

It's interesting that loyalty is in inverted commas. Perhaps this hints at a contempt for unionism in the mind of the author of the report. Perhaps being given the job of finding a way to expel Catholics from Northern Ireland would incline you towards thinking ill of those on whose behalf it was to be done.

The report continues: 'Though financial inducement could overcome some of the reluctance, it is doubtful whether the cohesive and large Catholic population of Belfast would agree to move; the matter would for them be as much of principle as of economics.'

I would think that, more than economics or principle, they would have been horrified at the sheer inconvenience of it. I was of one of those families in west Belfast that would have been moved had this idea ever been adopted, and we had no notion that the British were discussing how we were to be relocated and our house given to a Protestant family from

Newry or Derry, how our objections were to be met, where we were to be put and how much compensation we would be paid. I was going to leave anyway. I suspect that if they had offered my father a home in Derry, having already transferred Derry to the Republic, and accompanied the offer with an awful lot of money, he might have been interested. But, as the report already acknowledges, we weren't the problem, the IRA was.

We would have seen our transfer out of Northern Ireland as part of a collective punishment, as the government adopting the strategy of the loyalist paramilitaries who were already driving Catholics from their homes in mixed areas. And the IRA would simply have said, with some plausibility, that the days of the Penal Laws were back. They would have invoked memories of Cromwell and Henry VIII and would have enjoyed an enhanced rationale for war.

The job of getting people to move, if they were disinclined to, would have fallen to the British Army, which was already on the streets. The report asks: 'If voluntary and induced movement failed, would compulsion be practicable? It would raise in an even more acute form the definition of who should move. It is difficult to conceive a sure way of ascertaining the political views of a person who is unwilling to take the action which that information is designed to facilitate.'

I marvel at the elegance of that phrasing. It seems indicative of feigned patience in one who has been asked to consider an impractical idea and yet has to treat the request seriously and respond logically, rather than simply scoff at it, because the person who has raised the question is the prime minister.

One tries to imagine armed soldiers at the door requiring to know whether our political allegiances entitled us to stay in our home and inevitably resorting to force when we rejected their right even to ask such a question. Clearing the housing estates of west Belfast and Derry would have been impossible without awful violence.

It wouldn't have been a matter of a nice official coming to the door to tell us that our removal men were ready. There wouldn't have been enough removal vans in the country to cope with the numbers being moved. As we were leaving our homes, all of our neighbours would be moving too, and people in all of the neighbouring streets and housing estates across half of Belfast, and the same happening in Derry and Newry and Omagh and Armagh, all over the place.

They would not have been able to put us on trains, even if we were happy to go, so they would have had to put us in transit camps. The state had already had huge logistical problems the previous year interning 300 men. It simply hadn't the resources to move 300,000 men, women and children.

What was it to do then? Confine us to our neighbourhoods and make the transfer over a period of months and years? The entire object of the plan was to contain and remove the threat from the IRA, yet such measures could only have amplified it.

The authors of the report did not have to contemplate that horror because it was already clear to them that the whole idea was untenable and illegal: 'Forced movement would moreover be a breach of Article 3(1) of the 4th Protocol of the European Convention ("… no one shall be expelled … from the territory of the State of which he is a national").'

And what of the European Union, or the EEC, the European Economic Community, as it was then? Britain and Ireland were joining at the same time. At a summit with the Taoiseach Jack

Lynch in September 1971, Prime Minister Edward Heath had expressed a hope that the neighbouring countries would not have to carry their unresolved difficulties into the larger forum. That was too much to hope for, but redrawing the border and shifting populations would have created inconceivable problems for the Community. Our new partners in Germany and France already knew all about mass deportations, or ethnic cleansing as it has come to be known, and the long-term impressions left on people who suffer them.

And how were those uprooted people to be stopped from coming back?

> Any transfer of population, however accomplished, would be helpful only to the extent that it was permanent. To keep out of Northern Ireland those who had been transferred, a formidable barrier of control (including immigration controls) would have to be erected, not only on the new Border but also between the Republic and Great Britain. The administrative burden would be considerable; and HMG would also be in breach of its obligation to the EEC on the free movement of labour.

And if that didn't make the point clearly the eloquent official drove it home:

> In the Irish Republic opposition would be vehement and universal. Any reversal of the present policy of reconciliation, and the adoption of a policy of demarcation and compulsory ghettos, would emphasise in the crudest terms the present division in Ireland. It

would show the utter failure of [Taoiseach] Mr. Lynch's policy of trusting the British, and his fall must be considered likely. A successor government would echo the hawkish sentiments of most Irishmen, and increased IRA activity from the South would ensue. Appeals to the UN, Strasbourg, etc., seem inevitable.

But the likely response of the Irish Republic was not the only worry. The world would see Britain as having taken sides in a sectarian civil war: 'Any faint hope of success must be set against the implications of a course which would demonstrate to the world that HMG was unable to bring about the peaceable solution of problems save by expelling large numbers of its own citizens and doing so on a religious basis.'

The report did however suggest a 'possible palliative' if the transfers of populations and territory went ahead. This idea was 'to put the transferred territory into limbo and announce that those residing therein would still be considered part of the Northern Ireland electorate for any Plebiscite on the continuance of Northern Ireland as part of the UK'.

Having comprehensively demolished the idea of redrawing the border and moving all northern Catholics to the other side of it, the report touches briefly on an alternative it was not asked to consider: 'The ceding of smaller parts of Northern Ireland where there is a large Catholic majority (e.g. Newry, Londonderry) as one element in a settlement raises a different range of consideration [sic] and has not been examined in this Appendix.'

When the conference anticipated in this report went ahead in September 1972, the Irish government did not attend.

Neither did the SDLP. Some unionists who were invited also stayed away. The British brought a proposal that nationalists in Northern Ireland, far from being expelled, should have a share of executive power and that there should be something called an Irish Dimension. But Northern Ireland would be Northern Ireland as long as the majority there wanted that.

The report killed off any consideration then of repartition and a complete and final separation of the two communities. It appears that Margaret Thatcher had not read it, but her advisors and diplomats were able to politely slap down her own suggestion of repartition without having to go into the detail of what it would involve. She raised the idea at a meeting at Chequers in the early 1980s, in the early stages of negotiations towards the Anglo-Irish Agreement of 1985. She wasn't just throwing out a wild idea but had already received a briefing paper setting out the ideas of Dr Paul Compton of Queen's University on how the border could be redrawn and parts of Belfast might be walled off and connected to the Republic through a land corridor. However, much work had gone into preparing that paper, the idea was quickly dismissed.

David Goodall was one of the diplomats dealing with the Irish government at that time. Thatcher nicknamed him 'the Clergyman'. His job was to speak calm sense to her occasional flurries of fanatical thinking. 'Discussion took place in the Long Gallery [at Chequers] round a log fire which the Prime Minister kept restlessly getting up to poke and replenish.' (Goodall, 2020.)

At that meeting, Philip Woodfield also joined the discussions. He had been on the delegation that had negotiated the IRA ceasefire of 1972 with Gerry Adams and Dáithí Ó

Conaill and, as one of the officials close to the preparations for the Darlington Conference, may even have been the author of the dismissive 1972 report. Goodall says they allowed Thatcher to 'purge her irritation' with proposals for population shifts and a redrawn border. He credits Woodfield with 'balancing gloomier misgivings' with an 'admirably dry wit'.

*

There is one crucial difference between any possible future repartition plan and those that were considered by Heath and Thatcher. They were looking on it as a means of establishing peace in a time of conflict, while future plans might be conceivable against a background of relative stability and by agreement.

Heath had asked for a report on how repartition and a transfer of population might be 'in harmony with military objectives'. Might it be achievable for political objectives alone? In such a scenario, forced deportation of people would be inconceivable.

Resettlement grants have been offered in the past. In the early 1970s the Stormont government ran a programme to encourage people to move to the new city of Craigavon. My own sister and her husband took the grant and moved, but Craigavon never really became more than a clutter of disconnected housing estates and roundabouts between Lurgan and Portadown.

The 1972 report concludes by saying that it did not really examine the possibility of smaller parts of Northern Ireland like Derry and Newry being given to the Republic. This would only be possible if the people living there wanted to be handed over to the Republic and if that state wanted to accept them. So might future British and Irish governments negotiate an agreed redrawing of the border to bring large numbers of nationalists willingly into the Republic?

I don't think so. Any such change would restore the Protestant majority in the reduced Northern Ireland and that would outrage the nationalists left behind. They would be returned to the minority status in which they had previously suffered discrimination. Moreover, in those territories handed over to the Republic, welfare benefits would either change to the Irish levels or, if retained at British levels, would create the obvious injustice of neighbours with identical circumstances receiving different payments. The dole for the unemployed is much higher in the Republic.

Currently the state pension in the Republic is also higher. And as we have seen, there is division of opinion on whether Britain would continue to be responsible for those in a united Ireland who had already paid National Insurance contributions. It might be more amenable to paying those who had been transferred to the Republic as part of a repartition for Britain's benefit.

Such repartition would formalise a Protestant Unionist character to the new state and kill off the prospects of a border poll that could unite the whole of Ireland. So there can be no doubt that republicans and others who aspire to a full united Ireland would protest vehemently against such an arrangement.

And, crucially, it would simply replicate the conditions of the original partition of Ireland. That also, however, brings another thought to mind. If the concept of repartition is simply inconceivable now, can the original partition ever be discussed as anything but an injustice? How could one partition have been right and any further partition be wrong?

The thought experiment of considering repartition leads to the conclusion that Ireland really ought to be one. It doesn't, however, give us any clue to how that might be amicably achieved. The division between Irish- and British-identifying communities has endured and peace walls are still needed to separate them.

Polling in the Republic suggests that a majority wants a united Ireland but not enough to make significant sacrifices. In a Red C poll commissioned by *The Sunday Business Post* and published in November 2021, 60 per cent of people in the Republic were found to want a united Ireland immediately and 62 per cent said the government should start planning for unity now, but only 27 per cent said they would agree to changing the Irish flag, while just 35 per cent said they would change the national anthem, both being gestures which might, in some measure, placate the uneasiness of unionists.

Unification might lead to higher taxation and fewer than half, 41 per cent, said they would agree to that. Interestingly, barely over half of the Sinn Féin vote, 56 per cent, would accept a tax rise to enable unification, though a quarter of the Sinn Féin vote would agree to Ireland rejoining the Commonwealth if Ireland was united.

There was no majority, even among Sinn Féin voters (47 per cent) for supporting the devolution of power from Dublin to Belfast to enable the power-sharing arrangements at Stormont to continue. If voters were given a clear understanding of the cost of unification before a border poll it is possible that a majority in the Republic would reject it.

Neale Richmond, who wants a united Ireland, believes that that would be catastrophic for the project. A yes vote in the North would require more than the followers of Sinn Féin and the SDLP to support it. It would require middle-grounders, people who would make their decision on pragmatic grounds. 'If we [the Republic] voted against it, we would lose those people and I do not think we would get them back in a successive vote.' (The Good Friday Agreement allows for further votes seven years apart.)

Recent polling in Northern Ireland by the University of Liverpool and *The Irish News,* showing support for a united Ireland at little over 30 per cent suggests that the middle-grounders that Neale Richmond needs are not really interested. So is the whole discussion a waste of breath?

16

WHY BOTHER?

THE QUESTION WE started with was Can Ireland Be One?

Let's try another: why should Ireland be one?

Throughout this book we have heard a number of reasons. At the Ireland's Future debate in Cork Tadhg Hickey articulated one of the strong historic arguments for unity. He said that the South had pulled up the drawbridge and condemned some of its own people to discrimination and the denial of their nationality. He went a bit further and said that the Irish in Northern Ireland were effectively stateless, which isn't an argument that has to be engaged with since it is not true. They are not wandering helplessly around a giant airport. They have a choice of two passports when those who are stateless have none.

But it is true that a minority Catholic population in Northern Ireland felt detached from the nation to which it preferred to belong and that, as a minority in a Protestant state, it was disadvantaged and discriminated against. I don't think that sense of detachment is as strong as it was in my youth. We move freely around the island and are more contented in the North for we are not demeaned or discriminated against as we once were. When I told a Sinn Féin supporter I thought we had less to complain about now, she, like Tadhg Hickey, brought up the horror of our being excluded in the North from RTÉ competitions. I doubt she would go back to the barricades over that.

Many Catholics, such as my own family, came to Northern Ireland to be better off, to have enhanced job prospects, free healthcare and better housing and welfare benefits. So the argument that we were ditched into conditions worse than those we would have known had we stayed in the Republic does not stand up.

But even if it did, Northern Ireland's Catholics/nationalists/ Irish-identifying people – whatever we call them – are no longer a vulnerable minority inside Northern Ireland. They can no longer be oppressed and discriminated against by a Protestant state. They do not need Ireland to be united in order to have their basic human rights restored to them.

On the other hand, neither do unionists need to be protected by a border against the grisly reach of a Catholic Church that no longer plays such a dominant role in Irish society.

Some argue that Northern Ireland is a colony of Britain and needs to be restored to its rightful place as part of the Irish nation. Kevin Meagher deploys this argument in his book *A United Ireland: Why Unification Is Inevitable and How It Will Come About*. But while Ireland may have been an unhappy member of a Union, it was not a colony any more than Scotland today is a colony. Colonies don't send MPs to the mother parliament.

One could argue that the fact that there is a majority in Northern Ireland in favour of staying in the UK is contrived, a product of an unjust partition. But that argument has been superseded by the Good Friday Agreement, which allows that uniting Ireland requires a majority vote in Northern Ireland. Both parts of Ireland have assented to that, as have the paramilitary organisations in the North including the Provisional IRA. The British retain the right alone to call that vote, but a failure to do so when real prospects of success were obvious would face political outrage and legal challenge.

Another reason for Irish unity is to remove the North for its own good from the United Kingdom, or British Rule, as republicans call it. The Brexit vote reinforced that thinking. Northern Ireland as a whole suffers as a minority within the UK. A majority did not want to leave the EU. The assumption here is that northerners would be happier with their affairs being debated in Dublin by TDs with a variety of Irish accents than they could ever be with decisions being made for them in London.

British, or English, rule has been more acceptable at some time than at others. The original civil rights campaign, after all, was an appeal by northern nationalists to the British government to insist that the unionists governed to British standards of justice and democracy. Labour governments have usually been more considerate of Northern Irish concerns than conservative governments. But an independent Scotland would leave Britain more solidly conservative and much less attractive to Northern Irish nationalist and middle-ground voters.

A variant of the argument that Ireland needs its freedom from England is that it needs to honour the sacrifices made in the past to achieve that freedom. Much of the Irish sense of national identity is founded on the narrative of that struggle. But a difficulty with that narrative is that honouring and preserving it may be incompatible with the unity of the people. The assertion of Ulster Protestant/British identity is a refusal of that narrative as much as it was a refusal of the Catholic Church or 'Rome Rule'. So building a new Ireland according to the visions of past rebels would alienate the Protestant/unionist/British-identifying people who regarded those rebellions as attacks upon themselves and their vision of who they are.

Neale Richmond and Jim O'Callaghan say, forget all that. Uniting Ireland is not about the past but about the future. They say all sorts of creative accommodations may be possible to preserve the British identity of unionists. Sinn Féin's Mary Lou McDonald herself seemed to go along with that to some extent in the Mansion House debate, when she said that she wanted to honour the heroes of the past but not to be bound by their vision. Sinn Féin has shifted focus many times, though it would probably be uncomfortable admitting its serial apostasies. The party has adopted and discarded several different visions of a united Ireland, from Catholic to socialist, inside and outside the EU, allied to Libya and to Irish America, its one constant being the unification of the island.

Another argument for a united Ireland is that it would establish long-term peace. This was the view of Hubert Butler. He wanted Protestants in the South to see unity as being in their own interest and to agitate for it. It is the only vision of the future in which the old conflict is resolved, that is by a nationalist victory, secured by a demographic advantage and a democratic vote.

This argument says there is no prospect of a unionist victory or a stable accommodation. A unionist victory could only be one which somehow ends the agitation from nationalism for unity. This cannot be done through repartition. Nor does the history of power-sharing encourage faith in long-term stable and creative government. So why not a clear-cut answer to the Irish Question in unification of the island? And those who don't like it can lump it or leave.

Doug Beattie has said he would stay. Arlene Foster, a former leader of the DUP and First Minister has said she would leave.

The answer to this argument is that unification would not guarantee an end to sectarian tensions. These arose before partition, even before the Union, so there is no reason to suppose they would be settled once and for all by an end to either. That sense of victory being attainable through Irish unity may not just be pegged to a hope of bringing conflict to an end. Victory may be attractive precisely because it affronts and humiliates unionists. In a divided society, polarised communities seek to undermine each other. Indeed, it may be that some cling to the idea of a united Ireland or a sustained Union with Britain for no more deeply considered reason than that the other community abhors it.

One might argue that the future offers other prospective internal settlements that a majority of nationalists might be content with, confident that discrimination and the eclipsing of their Irish identity will not return. Even ordinary majority rule in Northern Ireland, the system of government that produced discrimination in the past, might work better now, as it does in other divided societies, for both nationalism and unionism would have to compete for coalition with middle-ground parties to get power, and that would prompt them to moderate rather than accentuate their differences and animosities.

An argument for unity made by Gerry Adams and others is that both parts of Ireland were damaged by their confessional cultures in which full citizenship rights relied on membership of a religious denomination. So the merging of northern Protestant and southern Catholic states into one would have prevented the excesses of both. A stronger Protestant influence in the South would have restrained the state from delegating so much of education, health care and social services to abusive religious orders. On the other side, Protestants would not have been able or perhaps even incentivised to discriminate against Catholics, who, being a larger proportion of the state than the Protestants in the Republic were, would have been better placed to assert their rights.

This feels like a strong and attractive argument looking back, but, like the argument for saving northern Catholics from discrimination, it no longer applies. Catholic Church influence has already been curtailed in the Republic by secularisation, while Protestant influence in the North has been diluted both by secularisation and the loss of majority status. So, again, a problem that unity might have solved has gone away anyway.

From John Doyle, Neale Richmond and Jim O'Callaghan we have heard the argument that a united Ireland would thrive economically. Their vision is that the old argument be set aside and that the simple, pragmatic course is to merge the two parts of Ireland inside the European Union and invite further foreign investment.

The first weakness in that argument is in the hope that the legacy of division can be set aside and that the unionists can be won over. That seems unlikely, though perhaps not impossible, if unity becomes inevitable anyway through demographic shifts and strong campaigning leading up to a border poll.

One may suppose that if unionists were to find themselves more prosperous in the new Ireland they would more readily adapt to it. But the transition to a thriving all-Ireland economy built on inward investment will be slow and we would have to cut back the Northern Irish public sector before private enterprise was ready to employ all those discarded civil servants. Look at what happened in the northeast of England after Mrs Thatcher defeated the miners and heavy industry gave way to the emergence of a service economy. That was traumatic, not a gradual and stable evolution that looked after those who lost their jobs.

Still, there were some who argued before the Brexit vote that leaving the EU was worth doing, even if it took fifty years for the new global Britain to establish itself. There have been many in the past who argued that similar sacrifices were warranted in the cause of a united Ireland. But it is hard to imagine that families who depend on public sector employment will vote themselves out of their safe jobs and pensions, even if the case is plain that a future more productive Ireland would be better for their children than an Ireland of subsidised pen-pushers and paper-clip counters.

In a united Ireland there would still be the option under the Good Friday Agreement of retaining Stormont, power being devolved from Dublin rather than London. But such devolution would be as vulnerable to one side walking out as the current arrangement has been. If northern nationalists decided that they did not want to share power with the unionists, they could simply leave and let Dublin run everything.

Yet power at local level is attractive. It creates jobs and provides influence and the opportunity for parties to grow, so maybe nationalists would be happy within a Stormont devolved from Dublin. Unionists have tried to make devolution work, more at some times than others, but they have needed it more than Sinn Féin has. The DUP base is smaller than Sinn Féin's. Without the Assembly it has only a couple of council areas and a few seats in Westminster, whereas Sinn Féin has a major presence in the Dáil and the prospect of being in government there.

Almost nobody is saying now that we should have Irish unity to preserve an ethnically distinct Irish state, though that is clearly what the founders of the Irish state wanted. My personal Irishness is not a single coherent thing. It merges with the Scottishness and Englishness of my cousins and forebears. When I travel to Glasgow and Edinburgh I feel as if I am still in my own neighbourhood, even finding those places more genial than some of the streets I walked through daily as a child.

When I was in Ottawa, at a book festival, I addressed an audience of people who had come out of Belfast and Armagh and Derry for a better life. A woman came up to me afterwards and said her family was from the New Lodge Road. That road is on a sectarian interface. When I have been there it has been to report on murder and rioting. She asked me, 'Do you know it? Is it nice?'

Seen from the air, 'From a Distance' to cite a foolish song, Ireland is an island that looks compact and green. This too easily leads to a kind of geographic determinism, the view that an island is a country and should be undivided. Tadhg Hickey was appalled as a child to see the North and South of Ireland marked in two different colours on the map. The injustice of partition is simply obvious to him. And often those who argue that Ireland should be a single self-governing nation state refer to the fact that we are surrounded by water, meaning that sovereignty has already been determined by the sea, its natural boundary.

This thinking belongs to a time in which the sea divides rather than unites. Dublin is about as near to Liverpool as to Galway for a crow, indeed closer since the wind usually comes from the west. In the past, a boat moved more smoothly and faster than a horse-drawn carriage. The evolution of transport may have influenced our sense of nationhood as much as the songs about past wars.

In Heysham in Lancashire, where the Belfast ferry used to dock, there are the ruins of a church dedicated to St Patrick, who is believed to have visited monks whose old stone graves nearby are now open to the wind and rain. It's doubtful that our patron saint had the same sense that we have of Ireland as a country apart.

Ireland houses a meeting of two ethnic cultures and has done for hundreds of years. Roughly, we call them Catholic and Protestant or unionist and nationalist. And, of course, new cultures flow into the island from several continents, but it is this historic division that challenges the idea that Ireland can be one. Reconciliation between the centuries-old cultures may be more difficult than between ourselves and the newer inflows.

There is a mechanism agreed in the Good Friday Agreement for uniting the separate jurisdictions on the island of Ireland and lots of different arguments for why it should be done, but there is no sure route to uniting the people.

17

FORWARD TO CONFUSION

CAN IRELAND BE One?

Yes. But it's complicated.

The people of the island can vote themselves into a single jurisdiction, creating a thirty-two-county sovereign Irish nation. And they may well do so in the next decade or so.

Ireland's Future and other nationalists say that they want unity by agreement, but a day may come when they can achieve it by demographic advantage, regardless of what Northern Protestants want.

And if unification does happen, there is the chance it might not be a happy marriage. Some experience suggests it will work out okay. A Protestant minority found peace and stability in time within an uncongenial Irish Catholic state. And since that state is no longer Catholic, assimilation should surely be easier for the Protestants of the northeast. But there is another geographic consideration which is not obvious from the air but can be understood at ground level: that these communities in the North identify with territory and govern it at local government level. Disaffected Protestants, absorbed grudgingly into a united Ireland have the potential to be a truculent enclave in a way that the Protestants of the South did not.

We can be too blithe about how the people who would vote against unity might reconcile themselves to it. Kevin Meagher, for instance, says it's regrettable that Protestants don't recognise the Irish flag as including them and symbolising peace between orange and green (Meagher, 2022, p. 133). But that's like saying the Irish-identifying Catholics of the North should recognise that the Union Jack incorporates the cross of St Patrick. The reality is that both communities have seen the flag of the other used at street level as a marker of territory in which they are not welcome.

For all that southern Protestants felt alienated by the revolution and lost many of their big houses, the main upsurge of violence against them was brief and may not have left the legacy of trauma and grief that three decades of Northern Irish violence did. That simmering hurt will resist assimilation.

And how well would Protestant unionist culture fit in anyway? At its most vocal and trenchant it comes across as conservative, chauvinistic and religious. It strikes many modern commentators and observers as simply eccentric. They see this ethnic group as one to be won over, brought into the modern world, talked sense to. I prefer to start by acknowledging the fact of their existence and the need to seek accommodation with them, understanding that if they are dismissed as foolish and irrelevant then, inevitably, they will object to that and become more difficult to deal with.

Still, they surely understand that they do not have the influence they had in the past, that their population is in decline, in real terms and in proportion to the rest of the population. And we have seen that they are diverse within themselves, so that a truly ardent core that would resent all around them might be much smaller than the supposed 'million Protestants' of ready cliché.

One day the British government, through the Northern Ireland secretary of state, will be obliged under the Good Friday Agreement to call a referendum on Irish unity when the prospect is judged to exist that it would be carried. Since the Irish government cannot risk being taken by surprise, it must logically prepare for this. It will have to seek negotiation with the British on the terms of the deal if it is not to be lumbered with the North without knowing, for instance, who is to pay for pensions and at what rate. Without prior negotiation it may find itself having to conduct its own referendum, at a date chosen by the British. This is a vulnerability it perhaps should not have conceded in the Good Friday Agreement negotiations, but it is too late now to get the rule changed.

The Agreement says that in Northern Ireland the vote delivers a mandate for Irish unity if 50 per cent plus one of votes cast are for it. That is a clause the parties might have agonised over a little longer if they had already had the experience of the Brexit referendum and the disruption created by a radical change being delivered by a slim majority.

On the other hand, to say that a greater than 50 per cent plus one vote would be needed to affect change would be to place a higher value on a unionist vote than a nationalist one, and the obvious injustice of that would hardly have been tolerated, least of all by those who were accustomed to expressing their umbrage by bombing London skyscrapers or shooting at the police.

While a requirement on the secretary of state to call a referendum when there is a prospect of success may read like a great opportunity for those who want unification, it might actually push it further back than they would like. It effectively means a referendum can be refused until the British government is confident that most voters in the North want a united Ireland. There is no prescribed yardstick for that judgement, only the common-sense likelihood that the minister making the call will play it safe. No secretary of state will want to risk being proven wrong by calling a vote too early.

It is also possible that a British government could call a referendum outside the terms of the Good Friday Agreement at a time of its choosing, as Prime Minister Edward Heath did in 1972. Then Heath's point was to demonstrate that there was no possible majority for unification and to remove the demand for a united Ireland as a plausible solution to the violence. But when one is called under the Good Friday Agreement, on the judgment of a British secretary of state that a majority is now ready for a united Ireland, the secretary of state's credibility will be on the line. Is it really conceivable that, having made such a hugely disruptive political decision, the secretary of state would ardently campaign for a result that suggested the call had been the wrong one?

I think at that point the British government would want to have negotiated a package with the Irish government, which the two governments would jointly commend to the electorates of both jurisdictions. The alternative might be a no-deal unification with protocols having to be worked out afterwards. The memory of how badly Brexit was managed is bound to alert them to what could go wrong. The question is whether they could avert such a calamitous repetition of past mistakes.

Theoretically the British would be obliged by the principles of the agreement to be neutral, to stand over their claim that they had 'no selfish or strategic interest' in Northern Ireland. In reality they would have moved closer to meeting a key peace process demand of Sinn Féin, which they had till then denied: that they be persuaders for Irish unity.

The simple incentive to keep this tidy and get it done in one vote would be that they might condemn themselves to going through the whole thing again every seven years until unity was either achieved or comprehensively wiped off the table. The only obvious way that could happen would be through a No vote in the South.

Negotiations with the Irish government would have to start before the moment at which Britain would be obliged to call a referendum, yet entering into these preliminary negotiations with the Irish, short of an inevitable majority in the North for unity, would be hugely destabilising. Unionists would realise that they were about to be dumped and there has always been a section of unionism which has threatened war when insecure.

The Irish would need those negotiations too, because they would be in no position to make demands of Britain after the issue was decided. So we are likely to see energetic political activism around the demand for a united Ireland colouring all political debate in both parts of Ireland, and a high degree of anticipation or apprehension, for years before the vote is actually held.

There will likely have to be at least three years of negotiation between Britain and Ireland before the border poll is called. Then the question put to the voters will not be a simple yes/no to unity. It will be a vote on the terms for unity as laid out in a British–Irish agreement or protocol. But protocols get challenged and some who want a united Ireland might vote against that agreement and campaign for a unity on different terms.

With Brexit, agreement was signed at the last moment, and moral pressure and the imminent risk of no deal obliged doubters to vote for it. One can easily imagine intense negotiations up to a deadline and a shaky compromise being sold as an historic breakthrough.

Another possibility is that Britain and Ireland would not reach agreement, but Britain would have to call a referendum anyway, as mandated by the Good Friday Agreement. That creates the nightmare of the Republic acquiring responsibility for six orphan counties without any alimony mandated from the previous guardian.

Even if the vote passed on both sides of the border, there would be a further complication. There would then have to be an all-Ireland referendum on changes to the constitution. Already, some diplomats are wondering how to cope if the border poll referendum passed but the constitutional changes were rejected.

None of this was thought out during the negotiations to the Good Friday Agreement.

That Agreement clearly presumes that a majority of people in the Republic already want unity, so doesn't accommodate the prospect that they might not, or that they might have conditions in mind which Britain might reject. Some have argued that a referendum in the South would not even be needed. Barra McGrory, a Queen's Counsel and former Director of Public Prosecutions in Northern Ireland, was quoted in a BBC report in October 2021 saying, 'There's no constitutional requirement south of the border, nor is it in the Good Friday Agreement. I'm always surprised by some of the articles I read in the media that there have to be referendums north and south on Irish unity.'

However, the constitution of the Irish Republic, Bunreacht na hÉireann, says it is the 'firm will of the Irish Nation' to unite all the peoples 'with the consent of the majority of the people, democratically expressed, in both jurisdictions in the island'. So there will have to be some determination of the will of the people in the South, though perhaps this could be done by a vote in the Oireachtas.

Even a narrow rejection of unity by the North would lead to instability. We would be facing into a further seven years of debate and contention, for the Agreement allows for the vote to be held again and again at seven-year intervals. We might suppose too lightly that those seven years would allow for a further demographic tilt towards nationalism, simply deferring the inevitable. Unionists, fearing the same might leave, or they might rally for more ardent campaigning. Who knows what exasperation with that might lead to or what calculations loyalist paramilitaries might make? Would attacking the South make voters think again about taking responsibility for a troubled region or might it make them think that uniting the country was all the more urgent to prevent war?

Neale Richmond foresees that a narrow or negative vote in the South, combined with a narrow vote against unity in the North, would disillusion the floating voters in Northern Ireland. They might conclude that they had committed their energies to a cause that had failed and might urge that, rather than enter a seven-year cycle of referenda, they would prefer to leave partition in place. Then, when called to vote again after seven years, they would seek to finally kill off the idea of a united Ireland for the sake of removing the question of unity from the centre of all political activity.

But what if, at the first vote, a majority in the Republic rejected unity but the North voted for it?

This would be traumatic for the nationalist community. Having voted for a united Ireland they would have no case to make for successive seven-year votes in the North. They could plead with the South to vote again, of course, or they could challenge the legitimacy of the southern vote, or they could finally reconcile themselves to making their future with their neighbours in Northern Ireland. Many people in Northern Ireland have already done that, as polls attest.

It would be a problem for the Union too, for it would be confronted with clear evidence that one member wanted out but had nowhere to go, like a spouse having sued for divorce but unable to leave the house, the new lover who promised so much having suddenly lost interest.

Doug Beattie made a claim in our interview, cited in an earlier chapter, that the ascent of Sinn Féin in the South actually threatens the prospects of a united Ireland, as it will scare off northern middle-grounders who might otherwise be persuadable. The problem for Sinn Féin, and the DUP too, is that neither can deliver a majority for the outcome it wants in a border poll. Each has to campaign for the referendum in a way that contradicts how it campaigns in elections. Sinn Féin commits to preserving the legacy of the Provisional IRA. Having led the Provos away from violence and into politics, it cannot now disown them entirely, even to gain political advantage. That sets a limit to its support.

Similarly, the DUP, even in amicable combination with other unionist parties, cannot deliver a majority against Irish unity exclusively from their own electoral base. The pro-Union cause would need more votes than all the unionist parties together can command in elections. Usually about 60 per cent of the electorate votes in an assembly or Westminster election in the North. The referendum on the Good Friday Agreement had a turnout of 81 per cent. So, about a quarter of those who voted for the Good Friday Agreement were people who didn't vote for any political party. Their motivation was presumably peace and stability.

The turnout in the Republic was only 56 per cent, suggesting a lack of passion for the same issue.

In the North the question of unity will be decided in the most trying of times by those who have least passion for it. They will vote pragmatically so they will need to know that the country will be stable after the vote. They will understand that sectarianism will not end with the unification of Ireland. In the new Ireland there will still be Orange parades in the North, outrageous bonfires and occasional riots. The difference will be that it will be the job of the Irish government to police them.

When they realise how hard it will be to reach a stable agreement they may think it isn't worth the trouble.

CONCLUSION

THE BORDER POLL is probably at least ten years away and a lot can happen in ten years. Every other poll is set within a context: the political, economic and global circumstances of the time, and these change. Ireland's or Britain's economy might collapse. Brexit might have proven to be a hugely expensive calamity, or it might turn out to have been the lucky break Britain needed before the EU disintegrated.

We don't know.

One day I will have to decide for myself if I want a united Ireland. I will not be the teenager who was moved by the sentimental poetry of Patrick Pearse. I will not carry the past with me. I will not commit myself to voting one way or another in a world that hasn't arrived yet and which in the last ten years has already changed more than anyone predicted.

I can understand why my father was appalled by the border that arrived to restrict his own movements as a child on a trike, playing in the summer sun just yards away from it. I can also understand – though I would never have had the courage to tell him so to his face – that his brother was glad of that border when he deserted from the British Army in 1943 and took refuge behind it. That uncle of mine was a determined republican for the rest of his life and would have scowled if you'd reminded him he was once glad of partition.

I grew up at a time when contempt for the border and a

determination to be rid of it were elementary parts of the cultural legacy of Northern Irish Catholics. I personally refuse now to be bound by such a legacy and insist on deferring my decision until I have read all the terms and conditions.

I will not vote on the constitution with less care than I would take in signing a contract to buy a car. I hope after reading this book a few others are similarly undecided.

BIBLIOGRAPHY

Books

Anderson, Benedict, *Imagined Communities: Reflections on the Origin and Spread of Nationalism* (Verso, 2016 edition)

Bartlett, Thomas, 'Ireland and India, Connections, Comparison and Contrasts', in Michael Holmes and Denis Holmes (eds), *Ireland and India: Connections, Comparisons and Contrasts* (Folens, 1997)

Bayrakli, Enes and Hafez, Farid, European Islamophobia Report 2018

Bury, Robin, *Buried Lives: The Protestants of Southern Ireland* (The History Press, 2017)

Butler, Hubert, *Escape From the Anthill* (Lilliput, 1986)

Casey, Daniel J. and Robert E. Rhodes (eds), *Views of the Irish Peasantry 1800–1916* (Archon Books, 1977)

Costello, Edward, *Rifleman Costello: The Adventures of a Soldier of the 95th (Rifles) in the Peninsular & Waterloo Campaigns of the Napoleonic Wars* (Leonaur, 2005)

d'Alton, Ian and Ida Milne (eds), *Protestant and Irish: The Minority's Search for Place in Independent Ireland* (Cork University Press, 2020)

Deane, Seamus (ed.), *The Field Day Anthology of Irish Writing*, vol. 2: *From Poetry and Song (1800–90) through Prose Fiction (1880–1945)* (W.W. Norton & Co. Inc, 1991)

Deane, Seamus, *Small World: Ireland 1798–2018* (Cambridge University Press, 2021)

Dunt, Ian, *How To Be A Liberal: The Story of Liberalism and the Fight for Its Life* (Canbury Press, 2020)

Fennell, Desmond, *The Revision of Irish Nationalism* (Open Air, 1989)

Goodall, David, *The Making of the Anglo-Irish Agreement of 1985: A Memoir* (National University of Ireland, 2020)

Harvey, Dan, *A Bloody Day: The Irish at Waterloo* (Merrion Press, 2017)

Higgins, Michael D., *When Ideas Matter: Speeches for an Ethical Republic* (Head of Zeus, 2017)

Holmes, Michael and Denis Holmes (eds) *Ireland and India: Connections, Comparisons and Contrasts* (Folens, 1997)

Ignatiev, Noel, *How the Irish Became White* (Routledge, 2009)

Kee, Robert, *Ireland: A History* (1980)

Lebow, Ned, 'British Images of Poverty in Pre-Famine Ireland', in Daniel J. Casey and Robert E. Rhodes (eds), *Views of the Irish Peasantry* (Archon, 1977), pp. 57–85

MacDonagh, Oliver, *States of Mind* (Allen & Unwin, 1983)

Martin, Peter, *Censorship in the Two Irelands, 1922–39* (Irish Academic Press, 2006)

McAughtry, Sam, *Down In The Free State* (Gill & MacMillan, 1987)

McEwan, Ian, *The Children Act* (Vintage, 2018)

Meagher, Kevin, *A United Ireland: Why Unification Is Inevitable and How It Will Come About* (Biteback, 2022)

Morrissey, Conor, 'Peace, Protestantism and the Unity of Ireland', in Ian d'Alton and Ida Milne (eds), *Protestant and Irish: The Minority's*

Search for Place in Independent Ireland (Cork University Press, 2020)

Nuttall, Deirdre, *Different and the Same: A Folk History of the Protestants of Independent Ireland* (Eastwood Books, 2020)

O'Faolain, Sean, *The Story of Ireland* (Collins, 1944)

O'Halpin, Eunan and Daithí Ó Corráin, *The Dead of the Irish Revolution* (Yale, 2020)

Orwell, George, *Notes on Nationalism* (Penguin, 1945)

Pearse, Patrick, *Collected Works of Patrick Pearse* (Phoenix, 1924)

Scheper-Hughes, Nancy, *Saints, Scholars and Schizophrenics: Mental Illness in Rural Ireland* (University of California Press, 2001 edition)

Shea, Patrick, *Voices and the Sound of Drums: An Irish Autobiography* (The Blackstaff Press, 1981)

Sutherland, John, *Monica Jones, Philip Larkin and Me: Her Life and Long Loves* (Weidenfeld & Nicolson, 2021)

Tagore, Rabindranath, *Nationalism* (Penguin Classics, 2010)

Waller, Bolton, *Hibernia* (Dutton, 1928)

Articles and Papers

Barrett, Alan, 'Debating the Cost of Irish Reunification: A Response to "Why the Subvention does not Matter" by John Doyle', *Irish Studies in International Affairs*, Vol. 32, No. 2 (2021), pp. 335–37

Doyle, John, 'Why the "Subvention" does not Matter: Northern Ireland and the All-Ireland Economy', *Irish Studies in International Affairs*, Vol. 32, No. 2 (2021), pp. 314–34

Emerson, Newton, 'No, the UK will not pay a united Ireland's pensions', *The Irish Times*, 10 February 2022

O'Carroll, J.P., 'Strokes, Cute Hoors and Sneaking Regarders: The Influence of Local Culture on Irish Political Style', *Irish Political Studies*, 2, 1987, pp. 77–92

Winter, J. M., 'Britain's "Lost Generation" of the First World War', *Population Studies*, Vol. 31, No. 3 (1977), pp. 449–66.

ACKNOWLEDGEMENTS

NO BOOK IS the work of a single individual and many people have an influence on a writer that they may not be aware of, even some that the writer may not be conscious of. I would like to thank members of my family for the information they shared with me and the corrections they offered. My brothers, Roger, Brian and Niall, and my sister Ann have helped, as has my American cousin John Lucic and my Scottish cousin Hugh Sweeney.

Over the years my thinking on this subject has been tempered by former colleagues, Bert Tosh, the late Terry Sharkie and the late Betty O'Rawe.

My column in the *Belfast Telegraph* and invitations to participate in the Nolan Show, Radio Ulster, have given me the opportunity to develop and present ideas which shape this book.

My nephews and nieces Fergus, Lily, Conor and Katie also helped.

I received patient guidance and help from Alan Morton, Chris Hudson, Davy Adams, Colin Harvey, Mervyn Gibson, Neale Richmond, Sorcha Eastwood, Jan Carson, Trevor Ringland, Doug Beattie, Claire Hanna, Wallace Thompson, Frankie Callaghan, Glenn Patterson, and friends at the Tyrone Guthrie Centre at Annaghmakerrig, Jen Donnery, Olivia Morahan, Sonya Kelly, Eoghan Rua Finn, Brenda Kearney and Judith Waring.

I would also like to thank my agent Lisa Moylett and her diligent colleague Zoe Apostolides, and Wendy Logue at Merrion for her valuable editing.

My particular thanks go to my wife, Maureen Boyle, who puts up with a husband who frets about Northern Irish politics.